GRACE

THE POWER TO CHANGE

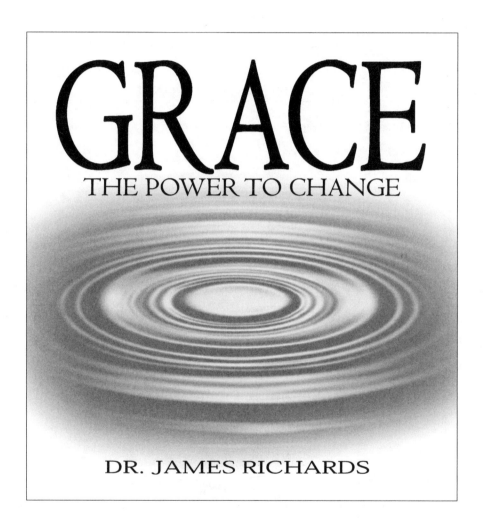

GRACE

THE POWER TO CHANGE

DR. JAMES RICHARDS

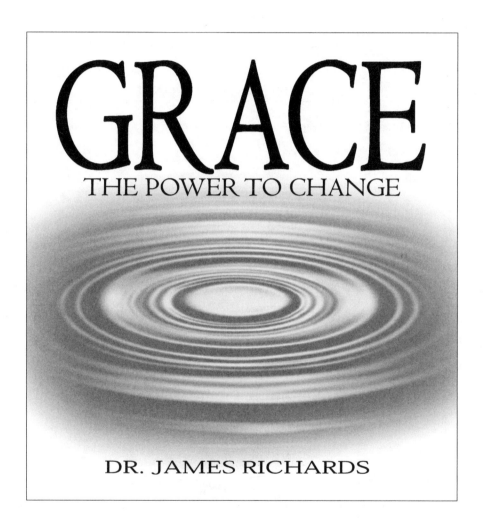

WHITAKER
HOUSE

GRACE: THE POWER TO CHANGE

For speaking engagements and ministry information, you may contact the author at:
Impact Ministries®
4410 University Drive, Suite 109
Huntsville, AL 35816
(256) 536-9402
www.impactministries.com
e-mail: impactministries@impactministries.com

ISBN-13: 978-0-88368-730-7
ISBN-10: 0-88368-730-5
Printed in the United States of America
© 1993 by James B. Richards

Whitaker House
1030 Hunt Valley Circle
New Kensington, PA 15068
www.whitakerhouse.com

Library of Congress Cataloging-in-Publication Data
Richards, James B. (James Burton), 1951–
Grace: the power to change / by James B. Richards.
    p. cm.
Includes bibliographical references.
ISBN 0-88368-730-5 (alk. paper)
1. Grace (Theology) 2. Change (Psychology)—Religious aspects—Christianity.
3. Christian life. I. Title.
BT761.3 .R53 2001
234—dc21   2001006151

3 4 5 6 7 8 9 10 11 12 ᴡ 14 13 12 11 10 09 08 07

DEDICATION

This book is dedicated to Robert Paul Lamb, writer, preacher, and personal friend. It was his encouragement and direction that launched me into the writing ministry. Because he helped me to write and publish my first book, thousands of people have been helped. Thank you, Robert.

About Impact Ministries®

James B. Richards is president of Impact Ministries®. This multifaceted, worldwide organization is pioneering an unstoppable ministry movement that is making an impact on the entire world. Impact Ministries® is committed to providing relevant, meaningful ministry to all nations, while equipping a new breed of leaders who are prepared to meet the challenges of the new millennium. To meet this worldwide demand, the ministry consists of:

1. Impact of Huntsville, a vibrant, cutting-edge, local church based in Huntsville, Alabama
2. Impact International Ministries, the missions arm of the organization that reaches the nations of the world
3. Impact International Fellowship of Ministers, a worldwide ministry base that trains, equips, and serves ministers to live their call while pioneering a new level of leadership
4. Impact International Publications®, changing the way the world sees God through books, audio, video, and other published materials
5. Impact Ministries®, which conducts life-changing seminars and outreaches in North America
6. Impact International School of Ministry, which provides one of the most unique ministry training opportunities in the world

For information on these and other services provided by Dr. Richards and his ministry team, contact us at:

Impact Ministries®
4410 University Drive, Suite 109
Huntsville, AL 35816
(256) 536-9402
www.impactministries.com
e-mail: impactministries@impactministries.com

CONTENTS

CHAPTER ONE

THE POWER TO CHANGE

One

The Power to Change

Probably the greatest frustration among serious believers is the inability to change. For the most part, Christians seem to keep their problems for a lifetime. This is not the will of God for the Christian; however, in most cases that is the way it works.

I have seen many situations in which individuals get caught in a trap and cannot seem to break free. For most people this is the major frustration in their walk with God. It does not have to stay that way.

When people are first saved, they usually experience an immediate change in many areas of their lives. Often, however, these changes are very short-lived. It seems that many believers fall back into the sins that had them bound before they came to the Lord. Beyond the obvious difficulties, this makes many new converts question the reality of their salvation experience. Whether or not we fall back into sin, however, can never be the means by which we determine the legitimacy of our salvation experience.

Then there are those sins we fall into after being born again. As an experienced counselor, I have observed that whatever takes hold of a new believer is seldom conquered. Once it becomes habitual, that problem is usually there for life. This is why we must guard our hearts above all else. If our hearts ever become corrupted with sin, that sin will seem impossible to conquer.

How does this corruption happen? Usually a person falls into sin through ignorance or unbelief about walking in the grace of God. Receiving and continuing in grace is the only biblical assurance we have of victory over sin. The apostle Paul wrote, *"For sin shall not have dominion over you: for ye are not under the law, but under grace"* (Rom. 6:14).

Grace gives assurance of victory over sin.

It is, therefore, this issue of grace that determines whether the Christian life will be one of joy, peace, rest, and victory, or one of difficulty, frustration, and defeat. If the new believer would continue in the Lord the way he came into the Lord, none of these problems would ever occur. *"As ye have therefore received Christ Jesus the Lord, so walk ye in him"* (Col. 2:6).

It Was a Complete Work

The greatest change anyone ever experienced in life came at the moment of salvation. In an instant, everything changed. That change came about by simply believing. The moment we believed God, His grace came into us, and we changed. If the greatest change came about because we believed, why not continue in that same simple believing? Or as Paul said in Galatians 3:3, *"Are ye so foolish? having begun in the Spirit, are ye now made perfect by the flesh?"*

In other words, when you came into this salvation, the Spirit of God did a work in you. Do you think that, now you are saved, you will finish this work by your own ability? The answer is obvious. No! Just as surely as you could not save yourself by your own efforts, you cannot bring about change through your own resolve. You are not saved by grace, then brought into righteousness by works.

When you came to Jesus, when you believed, God gave you a new heart and a new spirit. His Word tells us, *"A new heart also will I give you, and a new spirit will I put within you: and I will take away*

13

the stony heart out of your flesh, and I will give you an heart of flesh" (Ezek. 36:26). Your spirit was not only made new, but also made righteous, perfect, and complete. Your spirit was not made a little baby that had to grow up. God did a perfect work in you. Your spirit is as whole, clean, righteous, and perfect as it ever will be.

The need is not for you to become righteous. The need is for you to get that which is in your spirit to become a reality in your life. So how do you get what is on the inside to the outside? How do you get all that righteousness, holiness, and perfection into the realm where you really live?

Your Heart Is the Door

All that God has done in your spirit comes into your life through your heart. The condition of your heart determines what will come out of your inner man. When you were given a new spirit, you also received a new heart. Now, the heart and the spirit are not the same. There are different Hebrew words for heart and spirit, just as there are different Greek words for heart and spirit, and the functions of both are described differently.

God has given you a new heart.

The heart is the seat of your being. It is who you really are. The heart is the place where who you are in your spirit and who you are in your soul come together. All that God has made you in the new birth comes together with the thoughts, beliefs, and emotions of the soul. All this combined is the real you.

At the new birth, God also made your heart new. All the hurts and fears of the past were healed. Believing God suddenly became easy. You had new feelings about nearly everything, but for most people that doesn't last. Why?

Although our spirit man can be changed only by God, our hearts can be changed by our thinking. What we think, what we expose ourselves to, the beliefs we adopt—all affect and influence our hearts. Most of us manage to destroy the work God has done in our hearts, thereby limiting the life of God from flowing out into our souls and bodies.

Remember, the heart is the channel through which the life of God in our spirits reaches the rest of our being. Our spirits can be full of life, healing, joy, and integrity, but the condition of our hearts can keep those things from becoming a reality in this realm.

Losing the joy of our salvation, losing the victory over sin, losing anything that God gave us at salvation is not a reflection of the condition of our spirits, but the condition of our hearts.

Let me recount for you a story that I have heard hundreds of times. It usually goes something like this:

> I got saved, and everything was great. I felt the love of God. I was happy. It seemed like every time I prayed, God heard my prayer. Life was so exciting. Then, somewhere along the way, it began to change. I didn't feel the joy and peace that I had felt. I lost interest in reading my Bible. It all seemed to dry up.
>
> I went to talk to my pastor, and he said that, when I was first saved, I was a little baby Christian. God did those special things for me then because I was a baby. But now God expects me to grow up and mature. He expects me to stand on my own two feet.

This advice seems very reasonable and practical, but there is just one problem: You can't find this kind of advice anywhere in the Bible. You lost those feelings because your heart changed. God did not change; salvation did not change; the terms for salvation did not change—*your heart changed.* Thus, you cannot participate in what God has done for you.

The kind of advice that most people receive at this point puts them right into works and right out of grace. It is here that we start trying to get good enough for God to give us those feelings again. Thus, the emotional roller coaster ride begins. The more we follow the typical religious advice, the worse it gets. It's no wonder so many people just give up!

A Deep Frustration

The frustration of this dilemma is realized so dramatically because of the ultimate call of God. When God created man, He intended for him to live in His likeness and image. From that God-given identity and righteousness, man then would enter into an intimate relationship with God. It was only when man rejected the identity that God had given him that he lost the confidence he needed to have a relationship with God.

From the beginning of time, it has been the destiny of man to be conformed to the likeness of the Lord Jesus, through God's power, and to abide in a loving relationship with our God and Father. This is the highest calling of the believer.

This transformation is made possible only by the Lord Jesus. *"For whom he did foreknow, he also did predestinate to be con-*

Trying harder isn't the answer.

formed to the image of his Son, that he might be the firstborn among many brethren" (Rom. 8:29). Man was created with an intense need to be like his maker. David said it this way: *"I shall be satisfied, when I awake, with thy likeness"*

(Ps. 17:15). The born-again believer has a need to change into His likeness. No matter how we try to deal with it, cover it, or pervert it, the desire is still within us. It is a part of our new natures, and the Holy Spirit continually works in us to accomplish it.

For this reason, the desire to change is very strong in every believer, and that inbred need is a major source of frustration for many. When hope is deferred, the Bible says, it makes the heart sick

(Prov. 13:12). This is especially true when the thing we hope for is a change of character that will free us from those sins we have grown to hate. We desire to change, but it seems to be impossible.

People can mask this inability to change in many ways. Suppression, self-justification, criticism, legalism, and depression are just a few of the many carnal methods of coping with the problem. Unless a believer learns to receive the grace to change, his life will be full of frustration and deceit.

We Must Learn of Him

It has been my observation that most Christians want to change. They just don't know how. For many, the hunger for transformation turns into a lifelong struggle with the flesh that leads to a "works mentality." Although these people may lead moral lives, they still experience little inward victory. Their thoughts still rage within them. They even may go from seminar to seminar, or counselor to counselor, looking for the "anointed secret formula" that will set them free.

Real victory goes far beyond behavior and performance. Right behavior is of little value if we inwardly crave to act another way. Real victory is not walking away from sin, longing to give in to it. Real victory is walking away from sin with a deep sense of pleasure, peace, and gratification.

God has something better than "biting the bullet." It is not His will for the Christian's walk to be so difficult. It is His will that we change *"from glory to glory...by the Spirit of the Lord"* (2 Cor. 3:18.) Jesus said, *"Come unto me, all ye that labour and are heavy laden, and I will give you rest"* (Matt. 11:28). If your Christian walk has been one of labor and heaviness, it is time to come to Jesus. You may say, "I already have come to Jesus. I am born again; I know I'm saved. I don't need to come to Jesus." Oh yes, you do. You need to

17

come to Him and learn of Him so that you can find rest. Maybe you have met Jesus, but now it is time to *learn of Him.*

The children of Israel were a type or example to us. We can learn from their mistakes. Their major mistake was that they refused to enter into rest. They refused to trust God and allow Him to give them victory. He wanted them to enter the Promised Land. He wanted them to live in houses they did not build and eat fruit from trees they did not plant. In other words, they were to enjoy the fruit of someone else's labor.

But they would not go into the Promised Land. Instead, they looked at the enemy. They looked at the obstacles. They looked at the giants, and they said, "We can't do this." God knew they could not do it alone. He did not expect them to do it in their own strength. He said that He would drive out the enemy, but they didn't trust Him. As Hebrews 3:19 says, *"So we see that they could not enter in because of unbelief."*

The Israelites died in the wilderness of fear, frustration, and intimidation because they did not enter into rest. They did not enter into that place where they trusted God to do what He said He would do. Likewise, if we do not enter into rest (grace), we will die in our emotional wilderness.

> *Let us therefore fear, lest, a promise being left us of entering into his rest, any of you should seem to come short of it....For we which have believed do enter into rest, as he said...For he that is entered into his rest, he also hath ceased from his own works, as God did from his. Let us labour therefore to enter into that rest, lest any man fall after the same example of unbelief.* (Heb. 4:1, 3, 10–11)

Trust is earned; it is never given. We come to trust people as we become involved with them. As we come to know them, we start to trust or distrust them. In order to know someone, you must learn of him. The Israelites did not learn of Him. They didn't really know God. Moses knew Him, but the Israelites knew only about Him.

If you will humble yourself and learn of Him, you will find rest for your soul. For as Jesus says, *"My yoke is easy, and my burden is light"* (Matt. 11:30). If your yoke is not easy and your burden is not light, you have not really yoked up with Jesus. You have not learned of Him. You do not really know Him. You are still laboring in your own strengths and abilities.

As you get to know Him through a life of fellowship, prayer, and study of the Word, you will enjoy the transformation and renewal that you so desire. Instead of striving and trying with all your might to change, transformation will happen naturally. It will be like slipping on a new set of clothes. However, instead of putting on new clothes, you will be putting on the new you. The Bible commands us to *"put on the new man, which is renewed in knowledge after the image of him that created him"* (Col. 3:10).

The power to change is inside you.

You can change. The power to change is inside you. As you read these pages, you will find effortless change by the power of God.

CHAPTER TWO

GRACE—GOD'S ABILITY

Two

Grace—God's Ability

Traditionally, we have defined grace as "God's unmerited favor." Although this definition is true, it does not tell us what grace really is; it tells us only that it is free. One of the simplest definitions of grace I have found is "ability." Grace is *God's ability working in man, making him able to do what he cannot do in his own ability.*

Man has never had the ability to change his nature. Jeremiah asked this question: *"Can the Ethiopian change his skin, or the leopard his spots? then may ye also do good, that are accustomed to do evil"* (Jer. 13:23). All men are born with a sin nature, and no amount of good works can ever change that nature.

Under the law, people work hard at trying to change, but the Bible says righteousness never came to anyone by the law. The law did not change people; it simply gave them a standard of conduct. The weakness of the law is the flesh. (See Romans 8:3.) Now, when the New Testament speaks of the flesh, we usually misunderstand what that means. We think of the flesh simply as the cravings of the body. Although there are times when the Bible refers to the flesh as human cravings, it happens very seldom, particularly in Paul's writings. The flesh refers to man's ability. We are in the flesh when we try to change, perform, or become what we should be through our own strength and efforts. This is why the law did not work. It depended on the ability of man (the flesh).

Since man could never perform or obey the law in his own ability (the flesh), the law was little more than a source of awareness of sin. The law required perfection but gave no means whereby our natures could be changed. The law did not give ability.

Jesus Brought the Ability

Jesus came to give us new life. This new life is more than a ticket to heaven; it is a new nature that is born instantly in our spirits. According to Hebrews 7:19, 10:14, and 12:23, at the new birth, the spirit man is made perfect. That would be enough if we did not live in a body and have a soul. We have both, though, and God does not intend for us to be saved inwardly but stay the same outwardly. Neither does He expect us to change by our own power. He has made a way in the Lord Jesus for every person to be transformed. What is perfect on the inside can change the outside.

Grace is God's ability at work in us.

John said,

In the beginning was the Word, and the Word was with God, and the Word was God....And the Word was made flesh, and dwelt among us, (and we beheld his glory, the glory as of the only begotten of the Father,) full of grace and truth.

(John 1:1, 14)

Jesus was permeated with, covered in every part, and abounding in grace (God's ability) and truth. Jesus could walk in God's truth as a man only by receiving God's ability (grace). All that Jesus did, He did as a man full of grace. He gave us the perfect example of how a man could live above sin. He did it by God's grace (ability) that worked in Him.

You may say, "Great, that was Jesus! This is me. How will that help me?" John 1:16 goes on to say, *"And of his fullness have all we received, and grace for grace."* We are able to receive of that fullness of grace (God's ability at work in us) that was at work in Jesus. It is that grace that makes the new covenant life a possibility. Apart from grace (God's ability), we still would be striving in our own strength. We would be in no better condition than the old covenant believers.

Man had truth before Jesus came, for the law was given by Moses. (See John 1:17.) The law was truth. Man tried to live by that truth, but he failed because of his flesh (relying on his own ability). The flesh does not have the power to obey God. The flesh wants to fulfill only its own desires.

But grace *and* truth came by Jesus. Jesus did not bring truth alone. Truth alone would have simply been another law that man could not obey. When Jesus came, He brought us truth, but He also brought us *the ability to live that truth.* This is what sets the two covenants apart. The first was dependent on man; the second is dependent on God. The first brought glory to man for his accomplishments for God. The second brings glory to God because of His accomplishments in man.

Jesus enables us to live the truth.

Many who are trying so desperately to change read the Word in hopes that reading the Bible alone will help. However, the more they read, the more they are frustrated because they keep finding areas they cannot fulfill. Knowing the Word alone is not enough. We must know how to appropriate the needed grace to live the Word.

It's a Gift—Not a Law

We have taken Jesus' teachings and turned them into a new set of laws for us to obey. But His teachings are far more difficult to follow than the law. Jesus went far beyond the realm of performance;

He focused on motive and intent. Not only did He say that we had to do the right thing, but also that we had to do it from the heart.

When Jesus taught people about the law, He raised it to an impossible standard. First, He raised it to the level of the heart. He made the religious world see that God didn't just want right performance; He wanted a right heart. Second, He established that the motive of the heart always had to be love. No other motive would be acceptable.

Jesus was not actually a teacher of the new covenant. He was a teacher of the law. He taught of a new covenant that would come, a covenant that would be better than the first. This covenant would bring rest to a tormented soul, not more torment. This covenant would be a covenant that God would establish, and it would give the ability to perform. That is what makes this covenant such good news. God does the work; we believe and receive.

When Jesus talked about how hard it would be to enter the kingdom of God, He was not talking about how difficult it would be to get saved or to get into heaven. The call of salvation is to *"whosoever believeth"* (John 3:16). The call of salvation says that if you are weary and heavy laden, come, and He *"will give you rest"* (Matt. 11:28). It seems like a contradiction when He invites you to come but talks about the difficulty of entering into the kingdom of heaven.

The kingdom of heaven and the kingdom of God are the same thing. A quick glance at the Gospels reveals that the terminology was changed based on to whom they were writing. The kingdom of God was established when Jesus rose from the dead and established the new covenant in His blood.

The difficulty in entering the kingdom of God comes for those who will not accept grace and righteousness as a free gift from God. Those who take Jesus' teachings and make them a new law will struggle more than those who were under Moses' law.

Dependency on Jesus

One of the greatest frustrations for full gospel believers is knowing all the teachings and promises of Jesus, yet not being able to get them to work. Knowledge brings fulfillment only when we can put it into practice. Knowledge that cannot be put into practice will ultimately cause a denial of the truth. Thus, it is essential to receive the grace to walk in what we know.

Jesus is the Source of life—the Source of praise.

The Word will work in us only by the grace of God. Jesus' yoke becomes easy when I allow Him to do the work and simply walk along beside Him. When He does the work, I am drawn into a close, loving, appreciative dependency on Him. This dependency on Him is the basis of a relationship that never grows old or legalistic.

Because I am dependent on Him, He becomes the source of my praise. He becomes the source of my life. My thoughts, actions, and attitudes revolve around Him. Jesus Himself becomes the focal point of this life and eternity. Before men, I acknowledge Him for His grace, love, and mercy. Before God, He becomes my source of confidence, peace, joy, and praise. Apart from the grace of the Lord Jesus, I can never come into the all-consuming personal relationship the Bible calls for. However, in the fullness of His grace, He becomes my all in all.

Therefore, I will receive the ability of God. I will allow it to work in me. I will put no confidence in myself. I will depend totally on the Lord Jesus and glory in Him. And I will not be ashamed of this hope I have in Him. He began this work, and He will bring it to completion. (See Philippians 1:6.)

CHAPTER THREE

THE GRACE OF JESUS

Three

The Grace of Jesus

J esus is the perfect example to the believer of what to do and be in every area of life. In His earthly life and ministry, He showed us two very important things: He showed God to man, and He showed what a man full of the power of God could do. Both of these things were accomplished by the grace (ability) of God that worked in Him.

It is so important for us to understand the humanity of Jesus. A wrong understanding of His humanity will limit all that God can accomplish in our lives. It is the humanity of the Lord Jesus that gives us a basis for the hope of victory. Failure to see Jesus as a man full of the grace of God will result in a failure to see one's self as a person full of grace as well.

Jesus Lived as a Man under Grace

One of the most perverted doctrines of the antichrist spirit revolves around the humanity of Jesus. Even during the time of the early church, there was such an attack on the actual humanity of Jesus that it had to be addressed by the early writers of the New Testament Scripture. Today, we see many overtures of that doctrine in mainline Christianity, and it is the basis of the defeated life.

The apostle John said,

Hereby know ye the Spirit of God: Every spirit that confesseth that Jesus Christ is come in the flesh is of God: and every spirit that confesseth not that Jesus Christ is come in the flesh is not of God: and this is that spirit of antichrist.

(1 John 4:2–3)

This involves more than just a proof to see if a person can repeat the phrase, "Jesus Christ is both Man and God."

The early Gnostics denied that Jesus actually became a man as we are. In response, John wrote that any teaching that denies the humanity of Jesus is under the influence of the antichrist spirit. Of course, that does not mean that an individual is not saved; it merely means that this area of his theology is under the influence of the antichrist spirit. Acts 10:38 points out that Jesus was a man operating under the power of the Holy Spirit, not in His own power.

The teaching of Jesus' humanity does not take anything away from the deity of Jesus. He was God in the flesh. He was the Son of God, yet He emptied Himself. (See Philippians 2:5–8.) Although He was divine, on earth He was emptied of the divine power He had while in heaven.

Why is it so important that we understand this fact? Very early in my walk with the Lord, I saw that this truth was the pivotal point from which I would defeat the devil or be defeated by him. When I see that Jesus operated as a man full of the Spirit and grace of God, I see the possibility of the fulfillment of John 14:12: *"He that believeth on me, the works that I do shall he do also."* If Jesus did all He did as God, then I have no hope of doing the same things. If He did it as a man full of the grace of God, then I, too, can destroy the works of the devil. I, too, can conquer sin and fulfill my call.

Jesus continually gave glory to God for the ability to preach (see John 8:28), work miracles (see John 5:19), and do all the things He did. He never indicated that He did anything by His own power or ability. If the ability was not His own, whose was it? Obviously it was the ability (grace) of God, which worked in Him. (See John 8:28.)

Jesus was not born with that ability (grace); He grew in it. Luke 2:40 says, *"And the child **grew**, and waxed strong in spirit, filled with wisdom; and the **grace of God was upon him**"* (emphasis added). As Jesus grew in the wisdom of God, He grew in His understanding of God's power working in Him.

If Jesus Could Resist Sin, So Can We

Putting all the miracles aside, there is one area, more than any other, in which we should understand the grace that worked in Jesus' life: Jesus was a man who never sinned. I have heard all kinds of debates about whether or not Jesus could have sinned. It seems pretty obvious that there can be no temptation where there is no desire of the flesh. (See James 1:14.) Hebrews 4:15 says, *"But [Jesus] was in all points tempted like as we are, yet without sin."* Jesus' temptation was no different from ours. His flesh desired things that were not the will of the Father. It was not a "fake temptation." It was *"like as we are."* If the temptation was real, so was the ability to sin. Jesus could have sinned like any other man.

Jesus could have sinned, but He never did.

How was Jesus able to conquer the desire to sin? Hebrews 4:16 continues with the answer: *"Let us therefore come boldly unto the throne of grace, that we may obtain mercy, and find grace to help in time of need."* Jesus went to the Father and received grace (ability) when He was in need. He agonized in the flesh just as we do. The Bible says He suffered when He was tempted: *"For in that he himself hath suffered being tempted, he is able to succour them that are tempted"* (Heb. 2:18). It was a struggle for Him as it is for us. Yet

He learned to draw from God's grace and supernaturally conquer the desire to sin.

Just as Jesus conquered the desire to sin by the grace that worked in Him, just as He fulfilled His minis- try by grace, so we can have the grace of God working in us, making us able. Jesus was our Pattern, our Example. He showed us how to live by the grace of God. He showed us what a person yielded to the Spirit could be and do.

Jesus' Source of victory is available to us.

Victory, peace, and power are within the reach of every Christian. Victory should be as normal for us as it was for Jesus, by the grace of God. But we, like Jesus, must learn to tap into the grace of God. If we are to have the same victory, we must use the same Source.

Jesus is our only Example. All that He did, we can do; for that same grace is in us. You *can* live above sin. You can become the person you want to be.

CHAPTER FOUR

WHERE SIN ABOUNDS

Four

Where Sin Abounds

Most of my Christian life I was taught inaccurately about the age of grace. In this dispensation, I was taught, grace *covered* sin. Grace was basically reduced to an unmerited favor that made it possible for God to overlook, forgive, and tolerate sin. I was taught that we should expect to sin, but God's grace was sufficient for that sin. After all, Romans 5:20 says, *"But where sin abounded, grace did much more abound."*

Although there is some truth in what I was taught, it had little to do with grace. God still hates sin. God did not save man so he could sin and *get away* with it; He saved man so he could *come out* of sin. He gave man the ability to conquer sin by His power.

Romans 6:14 says it this way: *"Sin shall not have dominion over you."* If sin has dominion over you, you still have a sin nature. Sin loses its dominion over you when you are born again. At the new birth, you leave the realm of law that depended on your strength, and you enter the realm of grace that relies on God's strength. Romans 6:14 continues to explain why sin no longer dominates the believer: *"For ye are not under the law, but under grace."* Sin loses its dominion because of grace, because of the availability of God's power. Grace, therefore, is not God's ability to overlook your sin; it is His ability working in you to deliver you from sin.

Don't Give In—Conquer Sin

"What then? shall we sin, because we are not under the law, but under grace? God forbid" (Rom. 6:15). We do not need to give in passively to sin and wait for God's grace to forgive us. We need to yield to God's grace *before* we sin. We need to conquer sin. Grace has to do with the ability to overcome sin—not God's ability to forgive sin. Mercy is God's ability to forgive. I thank God for mercy, but I would rather walk in His grace.

Even after a person receives the mercy of God, he tends to live under condemnation. Sin damages the heart, making it difficult for him to trust God in the future. Even though God's mercy is already extended to us through the Lord Jesus, sin makes us doubt God's love and His ability to forgive.

Most Christians have so little hope of overcoming their life-dominating problems that they have developed a philosophy that says forgiveness is easier than resistance. This lifestyle quickly and accurately admits, "I don't have the strength to conquer this sin." However, God never intended for us to conquer that sin in our own strength. To do that is to reenter the realm of the law (the flesh).

Thank God for His mercy, but walk in His grace.

When James told us to resist the devil, he prefaced his remark with this promise: *"But he giveth **more grace**. Wherefore he saith, God resisteth the proud, but giveth grace unto the humble"* (James 4:6, emphasis added). What does it mean, *"He giveth more grace"*? More grace than what? He gives more grace (ability) than there is power of sin. *"But where sin abounded, grace did much more abound"* (Rom. 5:20). It never matters how strong the desire to sin may be; God will give more grace to conquer that sin, which means there is hope for your situation.

Yet God gives His grace only to the humble. Humility is simply the willingness to surrender your will, your opinions, and your view to the view and will of God. The proud person may not be arrogant or even outspoken. He may be a quiet, shy believer who feels he must do everything in his own strength. He may never ask anybody for anything, including God. That man cannot receive grace. God wants us to submit ourselves to Him, draw near to Him, and depend on Him. As we do, we begin to partake of that grace. When we have received the grace (the ability) of God, we are then ready to resist temptation.

Real Spiritual Warfare

The Bible describes the warfare that goes on in the life of a Christian. Somehow many have totally misunderstood spiritual warfare; therefore, the war they engage in is not bringing them victory. Most Christians mistakenly think that their warfare is with the devil. Although he is most definitely our adversary, he is not the focus of our warfare. Satan is a defeated foe. Jesus totally and completely conquered him and stripped him of all power and authority.

Satan does not destroy whom he *will;* he destroys whom he *may.* *"Be sober, be vigilant; because your adversary the devil, as a roaring lion, walketh about, seeking whom he **may** devour"* (1 Pet. 5:8, emphasis added). He is not capable of devouring just anyone. He is capable of devouring only those who are not sober-minded and vigilant.

The Bible warns about being anxious, fearful, and weighted down with the cares of this life. We are told,

> *And take heed to yourselves, lest at any time your hearts be overcharged with surfeiting, and drunkenness, and cares of this life, and so that day come upon you unawares.*
> (Luke 21:34)

The word *"overcharged"* speaks of being weighted down. When our hearts are burdened with anything, we are no longer vigilant. When we fail to believe the truth, we are no longer sober-minded. In that state of dullness and confusion, Satan is able to attack and destroy.

It is much like the thief who lies in wait outside the bar room. He waits for drunken victims who are unaware of the danger and unable to respond properly to the attack. The weakest person can win against a person who is drunk and taken by surprise. Since Satan has no power other than deception and accusation, we are vulnerable only when we refuse to humble ourselves and believe the truth.

Therefore, the war that we fight is not with the devil, but in our souls. When we believe the truth, grace freely flows from us to make us able to live that truth. When we believe the lies of the devil, the lies of our friends, the lies of the past, or even the lies of the preacher, we are no longer sober. If something doesn't line up with the finished work of Jesus, it is a lie.

The devil cannot do what you do not believe he can do.

Second Corinthians 10:4–5 says,

> *(For the weapons of our warfare are not carnal, but mighty through God to the pulling down of strong holds;) casting down imaginations, and every high thing that exalteth itself against the knowledge of God, and bringing into captivity every thought to the obedience of Christ.*

The things we are warring against are the imaginations that do not line up with the Word of God—specifically the new covenant.

I don't have to scream at the devil to win this battle. I simply gain control of my thoughts and beliefs. In reality, every verse in the New Testament that teaches about warfare always talks about your own thoughts, beliefs, and emotions—not the devil. The devil cannot do what you do not believe he can do.

The things that make sin seem to be so strong in our lives are the way we view it, what we believe about it, and what we believe about ourselves. If I believe I am a new creation, then sin has no power over me. In fact, sin is a painful, destructive force that I will not give in to.

The Truth That Breaks Sin's Hold

I am confident that no matter how great the temptation, I can always get enough grace to deliver me. First Peter 2:11 says, *"Dearly beloved, I beseech you as strangers and pilgrims, abstain from fleshly lusts, which war against the soul."* When temptation comes, I know it is only an emotion that is working in my soul. Emotions are part of the realm of the soul. All I have to do to win over that temptation is change that emotion.

> **There is always more grace than there is temptation.**

The Bible says to cast that imagination down. I need to bring it in line with truth. If I want grace (God's ability), I must believe God's truth. One of the greatest lies of the devil is that sin brings pleasure.

For most people, sin is that list of fun, pleasurable things that God doesn't want them to do. Similarly, the will of God is that list of painful, difficult things that God does want them to do. As long as people view sin as pleasure, they will always be tempted to go back to it.

But when we realize that sin, though pleasurable for the moment, always leads to the most excruciating pain imaginable, it will lose its appeal. Usually believing just this one truth will totally break the alluring power of sin.

In trusting God, one must come to understand that God's standards are not some kind of test. Avoiding sin is not some kind of test. Every pain in your life right now is the product of some sinful action, attitude, or belief. God is not punishing you for doing those things; those things always bring pain. They cause you to function in a way that is contrary to how you were created. If people would simply be honest about all the pain that would come into their lives by giving in to a temptation, they would immediately lose interest in that temptation.

After I realize that sin leads to pain, the next thing I must do is bring the thought of that sin captive to the obedience of Christ. Since Jesus conquered all my sin, and since I am in Him, the question is not, "Can I conquer this sin?" The question is, "Did Jesus conquer this sin?" If He did—and that He did will always be the case—I can rejoice that it has no power over me.

> **God wants you to avoid sin because it destroys you.**

I have to fight the devil only in the areas that Jesus lost the battle. Since He did not lose the battle in any area, there is nothing left for me to do except rejoice in that victory and count it as mine.

So many times I've had this war rage in my soul. Everything in me was saying, "I really want to do this!" When I would acknowledge the truth that "I am free from sin; sin has no power over me; Jesus conquered this sin, and I don't have to fight with it," the conflict would end. I have never been able to commit any sin that I believed and acknowledged that Jesus had won the victory over.

How Strong Is Sin Really?

There are reasons that sin seems to be strong and powerful. The first one is the amount of attention focused on it. Many people trying to fight their sin only magnify it in their souls, thereby giving it more power.

Next is the amount of pleasure you associate with that particular sin. If you think about the pleasure long enough, you will lose sight of the destruction that will surely come. Man was created to live in pleasure. We gravitate toward what brings pleasure. Our problem is that we are confused about what really brings pleasure. Sin brings instant gratification, but never abiding pleasure.

The failure to be realistic about the devastation of sin is another major flaw in our belief systems. Sin always brings death—death to our souls (minds, emotions, and wills). It is not God's punishment that brings the devastation; it is violation of the way we are created. It's like putting sugar in the gas tank of your car. The people from Detroit do not come out and mess up your engine; its destruction is the result of a violation of operational procedures.

What you focus on, you gravitate toward.

As long as you think God is the One bringing you pain, you can find all sorts of ways to get around your part in it. You could justify why your sin is all right. You could convince yourself that God's forgiveness will overcome all the negative effects. Or you could just stop believing in God. Regardless of the defense mechanism you employ, the results still come.

Trying to win the battle on your own terms or by your own strength is, of course, the tragic epitome of the works-oriented believer. How could you ever win over something that you really want so bad?

The truth is that there is more grace, more of the power of God, and more of the power of righteousness in you than there has ever been sin. If you believe in the power of God as much as you believe in the power of sin, sin will never seem big at all.

Goliath was big when compared with David. But David was smart enough to compare the giant with God. Why don't you do the same with your sin?

CHAPTER FIVE

IN MY WEAKNESS

Five

In My Weakness

For the one who wants to live a godly life, the frailty of the flesh is so discouraging. Most believers have tried to conquer sin, but out of ignorance they have warred *"after the flesh"* (2 Cor. 10:3) and not the Spirit. They have tried to fight using worldly methods instead of engaging in Christian warfare. (See 2 Corinthians 10:4–6.) If you are one who longs for a godly life, I have good news for you—your weaknesses can work for you.

It is foreign to our minds to admit weakness. I am not talking about having an attitude of failure and continually focusing on your inabilities. The Bible says, *"Let the weak **say, I am strong**"* (Joel 3:10, emphasis added). Our confession should be of strength, but not *our* strength. Christ in us is our *"hope of glory"* (Col. 1:27). We have no expectation in our own strength, yet we have every expectation and confidence in the strength of God working in us.

The main thing that keeps us from receiving grace is our strength. Yet we are taught to be strong. We glory in our strength and abilities. We testify about our strength. As a result, we have only as much victory as our strength brings us.

Your Strength versus God's Grace

Christians fail to realize that they are as weak today as they were before they got saved. If you stay in your strength, you will end up in the same place you were before you got saved. I clearly remember where my strength got me. I clearly recall how bad off I was.

Just because I got saved, quit cursing and drinking, and dressed a little better than I had before didn't mean I had any more strength. If I depend on my own strength, which the Bible calls the flesh, I will end up in the works of the flesh listed in Galatians 5:19–21:

> Now the works of the flesh are manifest, which are these; adultery, fornication, uncleanness, lasciviousness, idolatry, witchcraft, hatred, variance, emulations, wrath, strife, seditions, heresies, envyings, murders, drunkenness, revellings, and such like: of the which I tell you before, as I have also told you in time past, that they which do such things shall not inherit the kingdom of God.

The works of the flesh are a manifestation or fruit of being in the flesh, just like the fruit of the Spirit is a manifestation of being in the Spirit. Remember, you are in the flesh when you are depending on your own abilities to change, to be righteous, or to be accepted by God. Anyone who depends on his own strength will end up practicing the works of the flesh.

Our best efforts will not save us.

The very effort we put forth to be righteous is the very effort that causes us to end up in these kinds of sins. When we put forth our best efforts, we are still in the flesh. When we accept who and what we are in Jesus, grace flows out of us and makes us able to live the life of Christ.

In Galatians 2:21, Paul revealed a commonly overlooked truth: *"I do not frustrate the grace of God: for if righteousness come by the law, then Christ is dead in vain."* The word *"frustrate"* means to neutralize. Although every Christian has the grace of God inside him, he is able to neutralize that grace (God's ability). How?

We are always depending either on our abilities or God's ability. There is no in-between. If you are trusting your ability, then you have neutralized God's ability. If you stay in your ability long enough, it will get you right back into the same kind of behavior you were in before you were saved.

This is what happened to the Galatians. They were saved; they had accepted Jesus; they were on their way to heaven. Unfortunately, they had no victory in this life, other than what they could produce in their own abilities. This is what Paul referred to in Galatians 5:4: *"Christ is become of no effect unto you, whosoever of you are justified by the law; ye are fallen from grace."*

Falling from grace is not losing the born-again experience. Falling from grace is when you leave the realm of God's ability. It is when you attempt to obtain righteousness by your performance.

Every Christian wants to live a godly life. But we should live in righteousness by the power of the righteousness of God that is in us. We should avoid a belief system that says, "My righteousness is determined by the way I live."

Too often we overlook all those "in Him" Scriptures in the New Testament. All we are to God, we are because we are *in Him*. Colossians 1:27, *"Christ in you, the hope of glory,"* is more than a cliché. The *"glory,"* among other things, speaks of the view and opinion of God. The only way I can ever be the way God says I am is by the power of Christ in me.

When I speak of operating faith to obtain grace, please understand I am not saying *I* have to make this happen. Faith is not a power by which we make things happen. Faith is a trust, a deep conviction, and an assurance of the dependability of God. I don't make things happen with my faith. When my believing is in harmony with God, grace comes forth.

Acknowledgment Leads to Empowerment

The starting place to receiving the strength of the Lord must be in realizing your own weakness and admitting that you can't do the will of God in your own power. We do not want to be strong in our power; we want to *be strong in the Lord, and in the power of his might"* (Eph. 6:10). Our natural power is useless in a supernatural battle.

In 2 Corinthians 12:5–12, Paul described his struggle with Satan. Paul realized his personal inability. In verse 5, he said that he would glory (boast) in his infirmities (weaknesses). Then he described his situation: a *"messenger of Satan"* was buffeting him (v. 7). His thorn was not physical sickness, but a messenger of Satan. The word *"messenger"* is the word usually translated as angel. Paul was under attack when he wrote this letter. His life had been threatened many times. He had suffered every imaginable hardship, and now people had arisen in the church who were challenging his ministry and apostleship.

> We need supernatural power to engage in spiritual warfare.

In the Old Testament, the word *thorn* referred to people. (See Joshua 23:13.) Paul could very well have been referring to the Judaizers who followed him across the countryside, stirring up conflict and persecution against him. He could have been referring to the demonic spirit that incited the crowds against him. Whatever it was, it was more than he could handle. He was totally unable to do anything about his situation. He sought the Lord three times for this thing to be removed, and God's answer came back, *"My grace is sufficient for thee"* (2 Cor. 12:9). This was not a negative answer. God came through for Paul.

Not every negative or difficult circumstance we face will be changed. However, victory does not always mean the circumstance changes. As often as not, victory comes because *we* change. We need the ability of God working in us to change us, strengthen us, and make us able to walk out the will of God in every situation. God never promised to remove us from the world, but He did promise to give us victory while in the world.

Paul finally realized that he did not need a miracle from God to remove the obstacle, but the grace of God to face and conquer the obstacle. Unlike many believers in our day, Paul did not think God had failed him. He did not give up when he did not receive the desired results, and he didn't quit because he got an answer other than the one he wanted. Paul sought the will of God.

Victory does not always mean that bad situations turn to good.

He wanted whatever it would take to have victory. He did not predetermine what it would take for victory; he was obedient to the Lord.

When the grace of God comes, we do not endure—we overcome. We do not maintain a defeated or negative attitude. Victory is not hanging on with a bad attitude. Victory is overcoming with the joy of the Lord. How often I've heard people request, "Pray for me that I might endure to the end." You do not need to endure to the end; you need victory to the end.

With this revelation, Paul boasted, *"Therefore I take pleasure in infirmities, in reproaches, in necessities, in persecutions, in distresses for Christ's sake: for when I am weak, then am I strong"* (2 Cor. 12:10). His weakness and inability were no longer limitations. Instead, they were an invitation to yoke up with Jesus, to let Him pull the load, and to walk in the power of His might. Paul realized God's strength began where his ended.

Paul had already experienced the law. He knew what his flesh was capable—and incapable—of doing. But he had been set free from his ability. Now he gratefully counted all his ability as *"dung"* (Phil. 3:8) in order to know resurrection power. Unfortunately, many of us have never accurately realized the limitations of our own strength. We think we are supposed to be strong *for* the Lord instead of strong *in* the Lord.

Notice that Paul said he had experienced these things for Christ's sake. This is not the result of unbelief. These are the things we face when we walk in God's Word. Take note also that Paul did not remain weak—he became strong in Christ.

Winning with Grace

Even when facing the greatest obstacles, we can overcome with joy. Survival and victory look alike on the outside, but that's where the likeness stops. A strong-willed person can endure hardships and appear to be winning; although there may be some self-righteous gratification, he will never have real peace and joy. He merely survives. But when we overcome by Christ's power, there is always joy. Whether we are conquering sins of commission, wrong attitudes, or limitations, grace always brings joy. That's victory. Often a believer overcomes a sin or obeys the Lord, but does so with gritted teeth. That is a sure sign of laboring in his own strength. Where there is no joy, there is no grace.

The Bible says, "[Jesus] *loved righteousness, and hated iniquity; therefore God...anointed* [Him] *with the oil of gladness*" (Heb. 1:9). Because Jesus committed Himself to what was right before God, He received not only the ability to overcome, but also the oil of gladness. There was no sorrow in any of His sacrifices or no regret at overcoming sin. Why? He did it in God's strength, which brought Him the joy of the Lord. In Psalm 100:2, we are told to *"serve the LORD with gladness."* This is very difficult when we are laboring in our own strength. But Jesus maintained gladness until the end.

Hebrews 2:9 says that Jesus tasted death for every man by the grace of God. I do not think that Jesus, in His humanity alone, could have faced the Cross. Jesus' ability to face the Cross, to become sin, and to endure the punishment was a work of God's grace. Remember, Jesus was a man. He felt all the physical pain that any man would feel. But beyond the actual pain of the Cross, He also had to face becoming sin and receiving the curse of the law. (See 2 Corinthians 5:21; Galatians 3:13.)

Prior to Jesus' crucifixion, He went to the Garden to pray. In the Garden, He said, *"My soul is exceeding sorrowful, even unto death"* (Matt. 26:38). He was facing the agony of death and separation from God. He earnestly prayed, *"O my Father, if it be possible, let this cup pass from me"* (v. 39). He was not trying to escape the Cross; just prior to this He had rebuked Peter and made it plain that He would stick to the purpose for which He had come.

Earlier, when the religious leaders had tried to capture Jesus, He had said, *"My time is not yet come"* (John 6:6). So why did Jesus pray this way? I believe two significant things happened in the Garden. First, Jesus had to determine if it was the will of God for Him to face the Cross at that specific time. I do not believe He was trying to escape the will of God. Rather, I believe He was trying to establish it. Once He had determined that it was the will of God to surrender His life at that time, He then needed the strength to do it. It was here in the Garden in prayer that Jesus obtained the grace, ability, and strength to face death on the cross.

As we face the cross of dying to self, we need grace. That grace is obtained on a moment-by-moment basis. We

Dying to self requires grace.

do not receive grace in advance for every situation of life; but on a daily basis, as we pray, we obtain grace for that moment. When we face difficult trials, we should acknowledge in faith what the Word says about us and receive grace for those situations.

Whatever your sin is, whatever your weakness is, that will become your area of strength. To whatever degree you are weak in any area, to that degree the grace of God will make you strong.

CHAPTER SIX

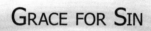

GRACE FOR SIN

Six

Grace for Sin

Any time we are in a state of lack, inability, or sin, we are in need of the grace (ability) of God. However, in these times of greatest need, our misconceptions about God cause us to run *from* Him instead of *to* Him. We feel we will be rejected if we run to God.

The Bible was written, among other reasons, to keep us free from sin. However, when we do sin, the Bible says that *"we have an advocate* [Someone who is for us] *with the Father, Jesus Christ the righteous"* (1 John 2:1). Since our Advocate is the Man, Jesus Christ, who has been tempted in every way that we have, He is a merciful and faithful High Priest who is touched by the feeling of our infirmities. Because He has been tempted, He is able to succor (aid, relieve, or help) those who are tempted. (See Hebrews 2:17–18; 4:15.)

Jesus is not repulsed by our inability to cope with sins. He knows it is impossible for man to win over sin in his own strength. Having walked this earth as a man, He knows full well that the grace (ability) of God is the only power that can make man *able* to win over sin. In light of Jesus' humanity, temptation, and victory over sin, *"let us therefore come boldly unto the throne of grace, that we may obtain mercy, and find grace to help in time of need"* (Heb. 4:16).

A Throne of Grace

"Let us therefore come boldly...in time of need." This seems like an impossibility. Our times of need are usually when we are being drawn into sin. Occasionally, our times of need are after we have sinned, and we lack the confidence to go forward with God. Whatever the case may be, our times of need are seldom times of confidence. Yet the Holy Spirit says, through the writer of Hebrews, to come before God *"boldly"* when we are in need.

How could one come before God with boldness when his desires are being drawn to sin? The answer to this question is the key to learning to receive grace for victory or continuing in sin. One of the great inhibitors to our boldness is the responses that people in our lives give. Although God is merciful and ready to forgive, people are not. We cannot let the responses of people affect our honesty before and our trust in the Lord. Though people may reject us, God does not.

First and foremost, we must realize that we are approaching a throne of *grace,* not a throne of *judgment.* Religion has painted such a mean, false picture of God that we usually run *from* God in our times of need instead of running *to* Him. Even under the old covenant, David's key to victory was His awareness of the mercy of God. *"The LORD is gracious, and full of compassion; slow to anger, and of great mercy. The LORD is good to all: and his **tender mercies are over all his works**"* (Ps. 145:8–9, emphasis added).

Run to God—not from Him.

Since it is a *"throne of grace,"* we understand that it is the place we go when we need God's ability. Often, we recognize our need of God's ability only when we realize we do not have the ability to handle things on our own. It is understood, then, that God designed it so we would come to Him in our times of need. Some religions would make us believe that we can come to God only when we have it all together. The devil (the accuser) whispers in our ears and tries to convince us that God accepts us only when we are faultless. But the Lord says, "Come to Me when you have a need. I will give you grace."

It's All about Jesus

Second, we must remember that we do not approach the throne based on our works. My works may affect *my* confidence in approaching God, but they do not affect *His.* The "works mentality" is one that says, "If I'm not worthy, God will not hear me." My question is this, "When is good, good enough?" No matter what you have done, the devil will try to convince you that it is not enough. If you pray for forty-five minutes, he'll say you should have prayed for an hour. If you fast for thirty days, he'll say you should have fasted forty days. If you read five chapters in your Bible, he'll say you should have read ten. But that is a "works mentality."

Even if you have done all good works and have not sinned, that will not bring you into the presence of God. Faith cannot be based on your personal accomplishments; it must be based on the finished work of the Lord Jesus Christ. As the Word clearly tells us,

> *Having therefore, brethren, boldness to enter into the holiest by the blood of Jesus, by a new and living way, which he hath consecrated for us, through the veil, that is to say, his flesh...let us draw near.* (Heb. 10:19–20, 22)

Faith that comes before the throne of God is based totally on the Lord Jesus Christ. The Bible commands me to base my boldness before God on the work of the Lord Jesus. Ephesians 1:6 says, *"He hath made us accepted in the beloved."* God accepts me before the throne because I am in Jesus. Faith believes it because the Bible says it.

Your emotions will lie to you. Feelings of unworthiness will flood over you, but that does not change the Word. The fact is this: you are unworthy apart from Jesus. However, it is not based on you. Acceptance is totally based on Jesus. You have His righteousness. If God rejects you, He must reject Jesus.

When I know I am accepted, I am able to obtain mercy. First John 1:9 was written for Christians. It is not a verse to be used in winning the lost. When I confess my sin, I find mercy and forgiveness. In the peace of God's mercy, I am able to apprehend His ability (grace). When I have His ability, I am able to overcome the temptation before I give in to it. If I have fallen, I can be restored.

Acceptance is based totally on Jesus.

Apart from realizing God's acceptance, you will never receive His grace. As long as you feel the need to earn righteousness, you frustrate the grace of God. But in understanding total acceptance, you can approach the throne with confidence.

Usually, the time we need to come to the throne of grace is not a time when our natural confidence is the highest. The two main times that we need help are right before we sin and right after we sin. Neither of those times would be a time of confidence if our confidence of acceptance is based on our performance.

We Are Righteous by Faith

"Therefore being justified by faith, we have peace with God through our Lord Jesus Christ" (Rom. 5:1). The word *justification* is related to the word *righteous.* A person who is justified has been made righteous. Only when we accept righteousness by faith will there be peace in our hearts about the love, acceptance, and approval of God. Without peace, we can never come to the throne with boldness.

Romans 5:2 continues, *"By whom also we have access by faith into this grace wherein we stand, and rejoice in hope of the glory of God."* Peace through the righteousness of Jesus is a prerequisite for access in grace. If you do not accept that you are righteous, grace cannot come forth to make you live in the power of righteousness.

A temptation is only as powerful as its effect on your emotions.

When your actions deny that you are righteous, you must maintain your boldness in who you are in Jesus. You must acknowledge your righteousness until your heart is established. Then the power of righteousness will fill your heart and mind.

It is not enough to have a doctrine of faith righteousness. You must believe it in your heart. One way you can identify what is in your heart is by identifying your basic emotions. The heart is the seat of deep, abiding emotions.

When I confess the Word, I am not trying to get God to do something; I am trying to get my heart back on track. I am focusing my faith. I am "stirring the gift" of God that is in me. I am persuading my heart in the truth.

Many times I have had temptations that seemed to be powerful. I would begin to speak the truth about who I am in Jesus, about the righteousness of God in me, and about my victory and freedom over sin. Suddenly, my emotions would change. I would feel righteous.

I have never been able to "give in" to sin when I was feeling righteous. Not only did I avoid the sin, but also the sin lost its appeal to me. The thing that looked so attractive, so logical, so reasonable, now looked ugly and undesirable. *"For whatsoever is born of God overcometh the world: and this is the victory that overcometh the world, even our faith"* (1 John 5:4).

THE MANIFOLD GRACE OF GOD

Seven

The Manifold Grace of God

We all are aware that we are saved by grace—or are we? In a recent Bible college class, I asked, "According to Ephesians 2:8, how are we saved?" Very quickly everyone responded, "By faith." Although that is obviously true, we are overlooking an essential detail. Ephesians 2:8 actually says, *"For **by grace** are ye saved through faith"* (emphasis added). It is actually the grace of God that saves us. Now, it is true that grace comes by faith. When we believe the truth, God's grace comes into our hearts and changes us. Faith brings grace, but grace brings change.

At the new birth, most of us limit God's grace to the forgiveness of sins. We do so because forgiveness is all we know to believe for. We are told that God will forgive our sins and take us to heaven when we die. Since faith comes by hearing the Word, we believe according to the amount of truth we have heard. Since we receive the goal of our faith (see 1 Peter 1:9), all we are able to receive from God is the new birth, which is obviously the most important thing of all. But though the new birth is the most important, it is not the totality of what Jesus accomplished on the Cross.

The word *"saved"* comes from the Greek word *sozo,* which means to save, deliver, protect, heal, preserve, do well, make whole, keep safe, or rescue from destruction. Although this includes forgiveness of sins, it is far more than the forgiveness of sins. *Sozo* speaks of all Jesus died to give us. It is not just a deliverance from sin; it is a deliverance from the results of sin.

Grace for Every Need

First Peter 4:10 speaks of the manifold grace of God. *Manifold* means various or many-sided. God's grace has many sides, facets, or dimensions. We should become good stewards of every dimension of the grace of God. We should have His grace working in every area of our lives in order to be established in all that Jesus has for us.

Faith brings grace, but grace brings change.

Since we use faith to get grace, and since faith comes by hearing the Good News of Jesus (Rom. 10:17), we need to hear and learn the promises of God in every area so we can begin to develop faith for that need. Keep in mind, God's grace is not automatic. It works only in the areas in which we operate faith. Faith comes only in the areas where we have heard the Good News about Jesus.

God wants us to have His salvation in every area of our lives. Because we heard and believed for forgiving grace, we received it. We received God's ability to do what we could not do in our own ability. However, God is able to meet the needs in every area of everyone's life.

The manifold grace of God can give you God's ability in every area. However, there is a process to follow. You must hear the Good News about what Jesus has accomplished for you. Then you must believe in your heart and confess Jesus as Lord of your life—including that area. God has the ability to heal you. He can deliver you from any bondage that holds you captive.

He has grace for any and every area of need you will ever face. But like the grace to be born again, you must believe in your heart and confess with your mouth God's Word regarding healing, freedom from bondage, or any other need that you face. Apart from faith, His grace cannot be obtained. (See Ephesians 2:8.)

Grace can be grasped only by faith. But don't get hung up about how much faith it will take to receive this grace. In most of Jesus' teaching about faith, He did not emphasize the need for great amounts; rather, He emphasized how little faith it took to get anything accomplished. Jesus told His disciples, *"If ye have faith as a grain of mustard seed, ye shall say unto this mountain, Remove hence to yonder place; and it shall remove; and nothing shall be impossible unto you"* (Matt. 17:20).

Many born-again believers are offended by the faith message. Usually it is because they tried it and it did not work, so they decided it was not true. After all, how many times did you try God before you made a real commitment? How many times did you dabble with "religion" before you surrendered to the Lordship of Jesus? How often did you go to church before you went to Jesus?

Faith does not happen because we *try* something. Faith happens because we *believe* something—something we find in **There is** God's Word, not something we merely acknowl- **grace for** edge, but something we believe in our hearts. Then **every** we confess it. Then we experience *sozo*. God's abil- **need.** ity to do what we could not do begins to work in us. There is an aspect or area of grace for every one of our needs. The manifold grace of God can make us able in any area that the Word promises and that we believe, confess, and receive.

About Faith...

Although I believe very strongly in many of the things taught by the faith movement, I believe the time has come for us to stop developing and using faith as a means to receive *things* and begin to use it as a means to receive *grace.*

There is nothing wrong with wanting things as long as we do not set our hearts on material possessions. God knows we need things. *"For your heavenly Father knoweth that ye have need of **all these things**"* (Matt. 6:32, emphasis added). We need things, but they should not be the goal of our faith. They should not be where we place our emphasis.

As born-again Christians, we should know that God wants us to have these things and that He will surely give us these things. But we should make it our top priority to *"seek...**first** the kingdom of God, and his righteousness"* (Matt. 6:33, emphasis added). The desire to be established in righteousness and the kingdom of God should be first. I want to use my faith to get the grace to change. I want character and integrity more than I want any of the things that bring pleasure.

I have found that a wonderful by-product of being established in the kingdom of God is that all these things will be added unto me (Matt. 6:33). I do not have to beg and plead with God; He is not withholding anything from me.

In fact, according to 2 Peter 1:3, I already have everything I need: *"According as his divine power hath given unto us all things that pertain unto life and godliness, through the knowledge of him that hath called us to glory and virtue."* God has put within me everything I will ever need for life. I do not need to get God to give me anything; I already have everything. As I accept and believe that, the grace to walk it out flows from my heart.

Proverbs 12:28 says, *"In the way of righteousness is life; and in the pathway thereof there is no death."* Too often we are trying to get the blessings of God to come to the place where we are. We want to abide in unbelief and have God deliver us from the effects of unbelief. It can't happen.

When I enter the way, the path, or the realm of righteousness, I find everything that pertains to life, and I avoid those things that bring destruction. It is the serendipity principle. The dictionary defines serendipity as "coming upon happy discoveries when one is not looking for them."

When I was a child, my brother and I walked to town to have an afternoon of fun. Along the way I found a small purse with some money in it. I wasn't looking for it; I found it on my way to do something else. That is the principle of serendipity.

The things that we are trying to use our faith to get can be found easier than they can be gotten. Taking a stroll down the

Righteousness is a free gift.

pathway of righteousness will expose us to all God has for a wonderful, fulfilling, abundant life. The confusion comes, however, when we think that we are talking about our righteousness. For the new covenant believer, the pathway of righteousness is not performance; it is accepting the righteousness of Jesus as a free gift.

The Gift People Trip Over

Unfortunately, when people get saved, they are rarely given the truth that will set them free. They are given the truth that will get them to heaven, but they are seldom given the truth that will set them free from the power of sin.

All we seem to emphasize is accepting Jesus as Savior. Again, though that is essential, it is more an end result than it is a cause. Most people accept Jesus as their Savior, then try to live a righteous life *for* Him. We need to accept Him as our righteousness; then we can live a godly life *in* Him.

Romans 9:32–33 tells about the stumbling stone of the Gospel: *"For they stumbled at that stumblingstone; as it is written, Behold, I lay in Sion a stumblingstone and rock of offence: and whosoever believeth on him shall not be ashamed."* At first glance, we think of Jesus as Savior being the stumbling stone.

A closer look reveals that Jesus as Savior was not the stumbling stone. Instead, Jesus as our righteousness is the stumbling stone of the Gospel. Read verses 30–32. They clearly reveal the source of righteousness as the thing over which people will stumble.

What shall we say then? That the Gentiles, which followed not after righteousness, have attained to righteousness, even the righteousness which is of faith. But Israel, which followed after the law of righteousness, hath not attained to the law of righteousness. Wherefore? Because they sought it not by faith, but as it were by the works of the law. For they stumbled at that stumblingstone.

All Romans 10 continues in this thought. Verses 3–4 declare,

For they being ignorant of God's righteousness, and going about to establish their own righteousness, have not submitted themselves unto the righteousness of God. For Christ is the end of the law for righteousness to every one that believeth.

When this talks about people who will not submit to the righteousness of God, it is not talking about people who are out committing gross sin. It is talking about people who are living right. But they are rejecting the only righteousness that is acceptable to God in favor of the righteousness that they trust in—their own performance.

As chapter 10 goes on to explain how salvation comes, it talks about a righteousness that is acceptable to God. Romans 10:5 explains works righteousness: *"For Moses describeth the righteousness which is of the law, That the man which doeth those things shall live by them."* In other words, if you want to be righteous by your performance, you must never fail or commit any sin, because the law accepts only total perfection.

I don't want that kind of relationship with God. That is the kind of religion (not Christianity) that makes people crazy. Mental institutions are full of people who have broken down under the attempts at perfection by performance.

Romans 10:6–8 begins to describe the righteousness that God offers as a free gift.

> But the righteousness which is of faith speaketh on this wise, Say not in thine heart, Who shall ascend into heaven? (that is, to bring Christ down from above:) or, Who shall descend into the deep? (that is, to bring up Christ again from the dead.) But what saith it? The word is nigh thee, even in thy mouth, and in thy heart: that is, the word of faith, which we preach.

Nobody needs to come and give this to you. No one needs to go anywhere to get it. It is in your heart as a result of Jesus' coming into your life.

Romans 10:9 says, *"That if thou shalt confess with thy mouth the Lord Jesus, and shalt believe in thine heart that God hath raised him from the dead, thou shalt be saved."* Salvation is the result of believing and confessing. But what is the cause of salvation?

Romans 10:10 explains its cause: *"For with the heart man believeth unto righteousness; and with the mouth confession is made unto salvation."* What brings salvation is the righteousness that comes by believing in the finished work of Jesus. A man *believes* unto righteousness; he does not *do* unto righteousness. He does not *perform* unto righteousness.

You may have believed on and accepted Jesus as your Lord, but have you accepted Him as your righteousness? If not, you are limited to the degree you can live righteously in your own ability.

Although there are many afflictions for the righteous (afflictions rise from the world when you live a godly life), I have found that God daily loads me with benefits. I do not have to search and strive to find them; I simply pick them up as I go. God adds them to me. The grace (ability) for things then becomes the by-product of the character (change) that is being worked into my life.

The highway of righteousness is lined with the blessings of God.

Therefore, in order to receive grace (ability) in all the different areas of life, I must accept in truth that I am righteous in Jesus. The manifold, many-sided, many-faceted grace of God works in the many areas of my life because I believe I am righteous.

CHAPTER EIGHT

GRACE IN THE HEART

Eight

Grace in the Heart

Thayer's *A Greek-English Lexicon of the New Testament* says that grace is a "divine influence" in the heart that does two things: strengthens and enables. Therefore, since the ability of God works in and from the heart, the condition of the heart is paramount when discussing grace. In fact, all that God does in us, He does in and through our hearts. *"For the LORD seeth not as man seeth; for man looketh on the outward appearance, but the LORD looketh on the heart"* (1 Sam. 16:7). Since God looks on and relates to us through the heart, it is essential that we heed the admonition of Proverbs 4:23: *"Keep thy heart with all diligence."* All that our lives are flows from the condition of our hearts.

Since grace works from the heart and is the product of faith, it will always be diametrically opposed to the natural mind. The natural mind does things in its own strength. The natural mind will always limit a person to the extent of his own capabilities. Therefore, few people ever fulfill the extent of their call or gifts.

The Natural Mind Leads to Destruction

"Eye hath not seen, nor ear heard, neither have entered into the heart of man, the things which God hath prepared for them that

love him" (1 Cor. 2:9). *"Because the carnal* [natural] *mind is enmity against God: for it is not subject to the law of God, neither indeed can be"* (Rom. 8:7). The natural mind cannot see or grasp what God has for us or what He is capable of doing through us. Even if it does, it is not subject to the law of God. In other words, even if the natural mind sees it, the mind cannot get it to work.

The natural mind is one that has been conditioned to reason everything out in accordance with the world's view. It has been trained to limit itself to this realm. It is a mind that is set on and considers things from the world's view instead of God's view.

Romans 8:5 describes the carnal mind as the mind set on *"the things of the flesh."* The *New International Version* says it is *"set on what that nature desires."* Being in the flesh, remember, is attempting to be made righteous by the works of our flesh. A mind set on works

"Works righteousness" doesn't work.

righteousness will stumble, fall, and be destroyed. *"The way of the* LORD *is strength to the upright: but destruction shall be to the workers of iniquity"* (Prov. 10:29).

A mind set on righteousness by works will produce a heart that tries to be righteous by works. This is what it means to be in the flesh. The person in the flesh always ends up in the works of the flesh listed in Galatians 5:19–21.

Besides a lifestyle that brings condemnation, a heart overwhelmed with works will never enter into rest; it will always have torment. Romans 8:1 warns against living in the flesh. *"There is therefore now no condemnation to them which are in Christ Jesus, who walk not after the flesh, but after the Spirit."*

The word *"condemnation"* means a damnatory sentence of judgment. The person who is trying to be approved by works will always expect the worst. He is always waiting for judgment. A person "in the Spirit," on the other hand, is always filled with hope, or a confident expectation of good. According to Hebrews 11:1, faith can come forth only where there is hope.

Only a heart permeated with grace will allow God to fulfill all His promises. The heart that allows grace to work in it trusts God and His Word explicitly. The word *believe* means more than mental assent. *The Amplified Bible* uses the words *adhere to, trust in, and rely on* to express a fuller meaning of the word *believe.* (See, for example, John 1:12 AMP.) Bible belief is belief that is put into practice and relied on.

Pride and Fear: Two Heart Products

Pride, like faith, is a product of the heart. The proud heart is unteachable and opinionated. Pride is always right in its own estimation. Haughty pride is easily identified. Opinionated pride, however, is sometimes a little more difficult to identify. Sometimes being opinionated is an overestimation of self, but sometimes it is an underestimation of what God can do in one's self. Either way, pride leaves a person restricted to his own abilities.

Since pride always says, "The way I see it is right," pride in its various forms is basically self-fulfilling. Pride leans on the "arm of the flesh." It looks at the promises of God and says, "I can't. I know what the Bible says, but I can't." Pride will always have an excuse for not believing God, which then becomes an excuse for not obeying God. Unfortunately, most of the church world accepts those excuses as humility. This is an arrogant opinion, a vain imagination that exalts itself against the Word of God.

Far from humility, all this reduces to evil unbelief. Hebrews 3:12 says, *"Take heed, brethren, lest there be in any of you an evil heart of unbelief."* The reason unbelief is so evil is quite simple. Faith is a response to God's character. It is the natural response for someone who believes God is honest. Unbelief is also a response to God's character—it does not believe in the honesty of God.

Actually, all unbelief is related to fear. The heart of the sin nature is not a desire to do evil. When I was lost, I wanted to do good. I just did not have the power to do it. I certainly did not believe that God would give me the ability to "live right."

Hebrews teaches that Jesus had to set us free from fear in order to set us free from the bondage of the devil. I believe the heart of the sin nature is fear. Because men are afraid of God, they will not trust Him. Because they do not trust Him, they turn to sin for gratification.

Faith is a response to God's character.

All lost people are in the flesh. They determine righteousness by performance; therefore, they live in fear. After all, when can you do enough to satisfy a perfect God? Unfortunately, most Christians never accept Jesus as their righteousness, so they, too, still live in fear.

We are all in the Spirit when we accept Jesus. Sadly, we do not *"walk in the Spirit"* (Gal. 5:25), or as the *New International Version* translates it, *"keep in step with the Spirit."* Therefore, we remain limited to the strength of the flesh and the fruit (works) of the flesh.

First John 4:18 tells us that fear has to do with punishment. When we determine our righteousness by our performance, we live in fear of punishment. We can't trust (have faith in) a God who we think is against us. Fear will not leave until we accept Jesus as our righteousness. Then faith (trust) comes, and fear is gone.

It takes humility to receive the righteousness of God. James 4:6 says, *"God resisteth the proud, but giveth grace unto the humble."* Humility is not a "cast down" attitude. Neither is it weakness. Humility is the place where you submit your will, your view, and your plan to the will, view, and plan of God.

As Christians, we do not have the right to have any view or opinion that is not in harmony with God's plan. To maintain any view other than God's is certainly the most arrogant pride.

Humility says, "If God says I can, I can. If God says I am, I am. If God says I have, I have." Then, in a heart of meekness and reverence, it depends on God to give the needed strength. Humility depends on God and joyfully gives all credit to Him for a job well done. When a life is changed or a miracle happens through the grace of God, all the praise goes to Jesus. Romans 3:27 says it this way: *"Where is boasting then? It is excluded. By what law? of works? Nay: but by the law of faith."* Paul wrote to the Corinthians,

> *But God hath chosen the foolish things of the world to confound the wise; and God hath chosen the weak things of the world to confound the things which are mighty; and base things of the world, and things which are despised, hath God chosen, yea, and things which are not, to bring to nought things that are:* ***that no flesh should glory in his presence****....That, according as it is written, He that glorieth, let him glory in the Lord.* (1 Cor. 1:27–29, 31, emphasis added)

It is the will of God that Jesus receives all glory because everything will be accomplished by His power working in us.

Since grace works in the heart, it produces change from the inside out. It is not something that we have to force or do in our own strength. When it comes from our hearts, it will be as natural as breathing. Because of grace in the heart, we can be and do all that God requires and still abide in rest. Rest does not mean we do nothing or become passive; rest is freedom from dead works. Rest means we do not have to work for righteousness or acceptance.

Because I am free from dead works for righteousness and acceptance, I can use my faith for righteousness. Then grace will bear fruit.

You obviously want to live "right." Now it is time to refocus your attention. It is time to focus on your heart.

CHAPTER NINE

GRACE THROUGH RIGHTEOUSNESS

Nine

Grace through Righteousness

We've already established that under the law, man attempted to be right before God in his own strength. This is called "works righteousness." The weakness of the law, however, was the flesh. (See Romans 8:3.) No flesh has ever been justified (made righteous) by the law. (See Galatians 2:16.) No one has ever been able to measure up in his own strength.

Now, in the new covenant, we have "faith righteousness." Although many people acknowledge this, few actually understand what it means or how it works. When we talk of righteousness, we usually think of morality, character, or actions. Though righteousness will produce these things, they are merely the fruit of faith righteousness. They are not righteousness in their own merit.

In Philippians 3:4–6, Paul listed his "works righteousness credentials." Then in verse 8 he said that he counted all that as *"dung."* He did not want to relate to God based on these personal accomplishments and moral standards; he wanted to relate to Him in faith righteousness. *"And be found in him, not having mine own righteousness, which is of the law, but that which is through the faith of Christ, the righteousness which is of God by faith"* (v. 9).

Jesus is our righteousness. He was completely obedient to the Father in life, death, and resurrection. The following Scriptures are just a few that clearly show that Jesus Himself was made our righteousness. Romans 3:25–26 says,

> *Whom God hath set forth to be a propitiation through faith in his blood, to declare **his righteousness** for the remission of sins that are past, through the forbearance of God; to declare, I say, at this time **his righteousness**: that he might be just* [righteous], *and the justifier of him* [the One who makes righteous] *which believeth in Jesus.* (emphasis added)

Romans 5:17 describes the righteousness as a gift. *"For if by one man's offence death reigned by one; much more they which receive abundance of grace and of the gift of righteousness shall reign in life by one, Jesus Christ."* Finally, 1 Corinthians 1:30 says plainly that Christ is made unto us righteousness. *"But of him are ye in Christ Jesus, who of God is made unto us wisdom, and righteousness, and sanctification, and redemption."* There are numerous other Scriptures about the gift of righteousness, but these should be sufficient to prove the Source of our righteousness.

We Are Empowered, Not Excused

The fact that Jesus is our righteousness does not free us from righteous living; it simply determines the Source of our power to live right. It determines what makes us acceptable to God. This is not an excuse to live an ungodly life. This delivers us from excuses for ungodliness. If righteousness is a gift, we have no reason to live anything but righteous lives.

We must keep in mind, however, that if a person does not believe in the power of righteousness by the Lord Jesus, that person will never experience it in the realm of practical application. He will falter through life, attempting to live righteously. Sometimes he will be successful; other times, he won't.

73

Satan tricks us into looking at our performance as the way to determine our righteousness. That puts us back under the law, and he always uses law to judge us. Once we enter into law, we enter into the knowledge of sin. With that knowledge of sin comes condemnation, fear, discouragement, and depression.

We do not need to look at our performance to determine our righteousness. We need only to ask ourselves this question: "Am I in Jesus?" If I am in Jesus, then I am partaking of His righteousness. I am not dependent on my own righteousness.

Remember, relying on Jesus' righteousness does not become an excuse; it becomes an empowerment. As I acknowledge that I am righteous, as my heart is persuaded about it, grace will flow out of my heart. Then I, like the apostle Paul, will abandon any trust in my past performance.

Paul realized that the result of abandoning works righteousness and entering into faith righteousness is knowing and sharing in the resurrection power of Jesus. It is that resurrection power that transforms us into the likeness of Christ. In Ephesians 1:19–20, Paul said that the same resurrection power that raised Jesus from the dead is the same power that now works in us. All this is possible only through faith righteousness.

Jesus' righteousness empowers believers.

We Can Have God's Quality of Life

The Bible says, *"He that hath the Son hath life"* (1 John 5:12), and *"I am come that they might have life, and that they might have it more abundantly"* (John 10:10). These verses, and the majority of New Testament verses about life, refer to *a quality of life*. The *Biblio-Theological Lexicon of New Testament Greek* says *zoe* (the Greek word for life) speaks of a quality of life as possessed by the One who gives it. Thus, becoming saved (*sozo*) means to receive the quality of life that God has.

Obviously, not every born-again believer is experiencing the quality of life Jesus came to give. The reasons for that are a lack of understanding (see Ephesians 4:18) and a failure to receive the grace (ability) of God. Grace (God's ability) will bring us into the *zoe* or resurrection life of Jesus.

God's grace can work only through righteousness. Romans 5:21 says, *"That as sin hath reigned unto death, even so might grace reign through righteousness unto eternal life [zoe] by Jesus Christ our Lord."* When sin reigns in one's life, it will ultimately bring that person to death. Sin always results in death. If we allow it to reign in our lives, we cannot experience the abundant life God promises.

On the other hand, when grace reigns, it will ultimately produce life (*zoe*), the quality of life that God has. Grace makes one able to receive that life. Grace makes one able to walk out that kind of life. Grace reigns in one's life through righteousness. We are under grace; it has been given by the Lord Jesus. However, it can reign as the power and strength of our lives only if it has a righteous heart through which to work.

Grace produces life.

A Straight Heart

So what is righteousness of heart? Just as there is a difference in being righteous and living righteously, there is also a difference between having a righteous spirit and having a righteous heart. Remember, our spirits were made righteous the moment we accepted Jesus. Our hearts, however, are righteous only when we believe the truth. Romans 10:10 says, *"For with the heart man **believeth unto righteousness**"* (emphasis added). This verse specifically talks of believing the truth about the Lordship of Jesus, about God's raising

Him from the dead. Only when one believes the truth of God's Word does he have righteousness of heart.

Although there are different words used for *righteousness* in the Bible, often when referring to the heart, the word *righteousness* means right or straight. We are right only when we see it God's way. Proverbs talks about unrighteousness as *"frowardness"* (see Proverbs 2:14; 6:14; 10:32), and *"perverseness"* (see Proverbs 11:3; 15:4) of heart. Commonly these words simply mean crooked. God works only in righteousness and truth. (See Ephesians 5:9.) Faith works only in righteousness and truth. Before a person can do anything with God, he must believe the truth. He must believe "straight."

It is fairly easy to believe the truth about Jesus. It is easy to believe truth about many things. The difficulty in believing truth comes when we read what God says about us. When we see how the Bible describes us, we spiritualize, dispensationalize, and "flatly deny" that we could possibly be what God says we are. A crooked heart does not believe what God says. Therefore, it cannot receive the grace (God's ability) to become what God says. Remember, grace reigns through righteousness. *"He that hath a froward* [crooked] *heart findeth no good"* (Prov. 17:20).

A righteous heart believes what God says about everything—whether or not it sees or understands it. Paul said,

> *Therefore being justified* [made righteous] **by faith**, *we have peace with God through our Lord Jesus Christ: by whom also we have access* **by faith** *into this grace* [ability of God] *wherein we stand, and rejoice* [joyfully boast] *in hope* [confident expectation] *of the glory of God.*   (Rom. 5:1–2, emphasis added)

In these verses, Paul acknowledged that faith provides access to God's ability. We have confidence to do this because we have been made righteous by faith instead of works. Paul went on to say that he boasted (rejoiced) in the confident expectation (hope) of the glory of God.

The Reality of God and Grace

All this makes sense when we understand the glory of God. In Romans 6:4, we are told that Jesus was raised from the dead by God's glory. This is what Paul was talking about when he said the power that raised Jesus from the dead is the same power that works in us (Eph. 1:19–20). Thus, the glory of God is working in me because the glory of God is what raised Jesus from the dead. But what exactly is this glory?

When we think of glory, we usually think of light, brightness, and splendor. That is a part of God's glory, though it is probably a by-product of glory more than it is a definition of glory. The word *light* is usually synonymous with truth. So we could say that truth always produces light, brightness, and splendor. However, the word *glory* in Romans 5:2 means the opinion, **God's view defines our reality.** judgment, or view, especially the good opinion that is reality. So the glory of God, which produces light, splendor, and brightness, is the view of God, which is reality. As a result, righteousness believes the view of God to be reality despite personal views or opinions.

So Paul said, "I boast in God's view regardless of my view. I am going to see it the way God sees it." That is truth and that is righteousness. In Romans 5:3, Paul continued, *"And not only so, but we glory* [joyfully boast] *in tribulations."* In other words, even in tribulations, when things look the worst, when there is no reason to believe the best, Paul said, "I'm going to keep joyfully boasting in my confident expectation of the view and opinion of God, because that is reality."

How *I* view it is not reality, how *you* see it is not reality, but how *God* sees it is reality. Unfortunately, we spend our entire lives making decisions based on our *perceptions* of reality instead of on reality. Thus, we never live in the reality of God's abundant life. When we see and believe it the way God sees it, we have a righteous heart. But remember, salvation (*sozo*) comes only when we confess the truth with our mouths. (See Romans 10:10.) So like Paul, we must confidently boast in the truth and reality of God's Word. When we follow this process in any area, God's ability goes to work in us in that area. That ability makes our confident confession a reality. A straight heart produces a straight confession, which brings forth the view and opinion of God. Therefore, grace reigns through righteousness (believing the truth in the heart).

Use Your Mouth

Paul's joyful boasting, or what some would call confessing, is very important to do during times of tribulation. Tribulation does not come to develop you or help you; it comes to destroy you. Your response to tribulation is what determines its effect.

When going through difficult times, it is essential that your heart remains stable and steadfast in truth. When your heart begins to waver, then to the same degree that your emotions begin to change, you will hinder grace from flowing out of you. Once you stop the flow of grace, you are limited to the extent of your own ability.

There are hundreds of Scriptures about the power of speaking. Confession, in the strictest sense, is to say something because it is in your heart. Often what we are saying with our mouths is not really a confession because it is not true in our hearts.

However, the power of speaking is clearly a part of persuasion. People are persuaded about Jesus because of the words they hear.

Proverbs tells us how we use our mouths to deliver ourselves from destruction. I believe that is the power of persuasion.

I have heard it said that the part of our brains that controls speech dominates every other function of the brain. I cannot prove that. However, the Bible says in James that I can turn my body in any direction with my tongue. (See James 3:4–5.) Proverbs tells me that *"death and life are in the power of the tongue"* (Prov. 18:21). Therefore, I will use my tongue to feed myself life.

When my emotions begin to deny the Word of God, I know that does not change the Word. I also know, however, that without consistent emotions, it will be difficult for me to walk in truth. When I realize the negative change in my emotions, I use my mouth to turn the tide. The words that I speak help keep my heart in righteousness, straight with the Word of God. Then grace freely flows from a heart that believes in the righteousness of Jesus that is in me.

Speak words of life to yourself and others.

CHAPTER TEN

THE BREASTPLATE OF RIGHTEOUSNESS

Chapter Ten

The Breastplate of Righteousness

Proverbs 4:23 in *The Amplified Bible* says, *"Keep and guard your heart with all vigilance and above all that you guard, for out of it flow the springs of life."* The heart is the seat of your being. It is the real you. All you are is a mirrored reflection of the condition of your heart. I cannot emphasize this enough!

Again, the heart is the seat of the emotions. It is the spiritual strength, intellectual life, and inner nature of man; it is the source of emotions, feelings, instincts, and passions. The Bible identifies it as the source of joy, gladness, courage, cowardice, fear, faith, love, hatred, and anger. In the heart, the Word of God is kept, the peace of God begins to rule, and God gives strength. In short, all that your life is, or has been, is the product of your heart.

Because the church has so little understanding of the heart, it has placed almost total emphasis on actions and externals. The church has tried to relate to God externally while God wants to relate to us internally. Everything we try so hard to accomplish by the "sweat of our brows" could be accomplished so much more easily if we would allow God to change our hearts. When our hearts have been changed, we do things because we want to. When we are driven by works, we do things because we have to. Grace does not just change the action; it changes the intention.

As we found earlier, *"A froward* [crooked] *heart findeth no good"* (Prov. 17:20). Proverbs 10:29 says, *"The way of the LORD is strength to the upright: but destruction shall be to the workers of iniquity."* Not only does God's Word not work for the crooked of heart, but it is also destruction for them. The crooked of heart are offended at the promises of God. His promise of a new identity and supernatural ability makes no sense to the carnal mind.

Real Righteousness Believes

In actuality, the promises of God belong only to the righteous, to those who believe the truth. There are many moral people who are totally unrighteous before God. If righteousness were a matter of moral living alone, then people could get saved apart from Jesus. Since man cannot become righteous enough to be saved by his own merit, he is saved when he becomes righteous through Jesus. In other words, he accepts the free gift of righteousness. When he rejects that righteousness and attempts to be made righteous in his own efforts, he remains unrighteous before God. Remember, an unrighteous heart is a heart that is not straight with what God says.

Isaiah 64:6 should give us an absolute view of our efforts for righteousness: *"But we are all as an unclean thing, and all our righteousnesses are as filthy rags."* Any righteousness that we could perform is just not good enough for God. It will not make us acceptable. It is a righteousness that comes by our abilities, not His. It is a righteousness that brings us glory, not Him.

It is also a righteousness that excludes people due to their inabilities. Works righteousness brings glory to the gifted and the strong, but it brings shame to the weak and incapable. It offers hope only for those who "can," but does nothing for those who cannot. The Bible says *"God so loved the world"* (John 3:16), not just the strong and capable. Romans 4:16 states this in no uncertain terms.

Therefore it is of faith, that it might be by grace; to the end the promise might be sure to all the seed; not to that only which is of the law, but to that also which is of the faith of Abraham; who is the father of us all.

Many morally righteous people who want to serve God are stumbling over the stumbling stone described in Romans 9:30–33. Then as Romans 10:2 says, *"They have a zeal of God, but not according to knowledge."* Romans 10:3 continues, *"For they being ignorant of God's righteousness, and going about to establish their own righteousness, have not submitted themselves unto the righteousness of God."* These people make their own righteousness their confidence before God. Since their righteousness is unacceptable, these individuals have alienated themselves from the promises of God. Therefore, the Word of God will not work for them. God's Word will work for you only in the area you believe it in your heart.

Righteousness not only believes God's Word will work, but also believes it will work the way God says it will work. Initially, Abraham believed he could have a son; he just did not believe it would happen the way God said it would. Abraham launched out in his own strength, and the way of the Lord that was meant to be life became destruction. Abraham's carnal attempt to fulfill the promise produced the Arab nations that live for the destruction of Israel to this day.

Belief is trusting in God's plan.

God did not want Abraham to have a son by Hagar. He wanted Sarah to bear him a son. In Genesis 15:6, we read that Abraham believed God, but it was not until chapter 17 that he believed it God's way. In Genesis 17:2, God basically said, "Now I can put the covenant into operation." Many people believe God can get you to heaven, but there have been wars fought over how that will take place. Righteousness knows that all God does in the new covenant is based on the finished work of Jesus.

Abraham, the Father of Our Faith

Abraham was the father of faith. He was the example to the Jews about faith—not faith in general, but the faith righteousness that was to come.

As far as performance was concerned, Abraham could be considered a failure. He failed at nearly every point. Things God said not to do, he did. Things God said to do, he did a different way. God told him to come out of Ur of the Chaldees alone; he brought his entire family. Even at that, the Scripture says plainly that it was his father who instigated that act of obedience. (See Genesis 11:31.)

When Abram left Ur, instead of going where he was supposed to go, he tarried at Haran until the death of his father. This caused him to arrive in the land of Canaan late; therefore, he was faced with a famine immediately.

Instead of abiding where God had led him, he went to Egypt. While there, he gave the woman whom God wanted to use to bring forth the bloodline of the Messiah to another man. Think of it! That is nothing short of prostitution for protection.

Also while in Egypt, he picked up a servant named Hagar with whom he later committed adultery and produced the present-day Arab nations. He wanted the child by Hagar to be the one who received the inheritance; God had chosen Sarah to bear Isaac. Ultimately, Abraham's compromise was so excessive that God made him send the first son away.

Throughout his entire walk with God, Abraham had to be reassured of his relationship with the Lord through supernatural means. Yet, in spite of all his failures, God called him righteous. *"And he [Abraham] believed in the LORD; and he counted it to him for righteousness"* (Gen. 15:6).

When we look at the context of Romans 4, we see that Abraham is an example of faith to us, not because he believed he would have a son. He was the father of faith because he believed what God said.

Romans 4:17 is probably one of the most misquoted faith Scriptures in the Bible. *"(As it is written, I have made thee a father of many nations,) before him whom he believed, even God, who quickeneth the dead, and calleth those things which be not as though they were."* This is not a Scripture about Abraham's calling *"those things which be not as though they were."* It is a Scripture about *God's* calling those things that *"be not as though they were."* The thing that "was not" was Abraham's righteousness. God called him righteous and related to him as righteous, even though he was not.

Abraham is our example of a man who trusted and related to God solely on the integrity of God's Word. Abraham believed he was a friend of God. Abraham accepted God's opinion of him as righteous. The primary difference between us and Abraham is that we are righteous! Abraham was only considered righteous. His righteousness was imputed to him. We have been made righteous by the finished work of Jesus.

Abraham, with all his failures, was still able to relate to God by God's definition of righteousness, not his own. Our greatest challenge of faith will not be faith for things. Our greatest challenge of faith will be faith righteousness. We all believe we should be righteous. We all know God requires righteousness, but we fail to believe it comes the way He says it does.

Guarding the Heart

A crooked heart may believe the truth, but that truth is slightly bent to that heart's own preference. That perversion of the truth is destructive because it will not work. God works in righteousness (straight). Since the Word of God is called light, we gain much understanding about truth by understanding light. When light bends, it changes colors. We have all seen small prisms hanging in a window. When the light shines in, it is clear and colorless. However, when that light is bent, it comes out many different colors. Likewise, the pure Word of God can enter into a crooked heart—a heart of prejudice, preference, or tradition—and be dispersed into an understanding different from how it came in. In other words, we can actually hear one thing and understand it to be something totally different from what was said. For this reason we must continually guard our hearts.

Ephesians 6:14 tells us to put on the breastplate of righteousness. The breastplate protects the heart. We must guard our hearts with God's righteousness. We should not allow anything other than the Word of God to enter our hearts. Neither must we expose ourselves to those things that twist or distort the Word in any way.

This is especially true in the area of righteousness. What you believe about righteousness will affect your heart more than anything else you believe. What you believe about righteousness will determine whether the Word of God will work in your life.

In Romans 1:16, Paul set forth an explanation of the Gospel and an understanding of how the power of God works: *"For I am not ashamed of the gospel of Christ: for it is the power of God unto salvation to every one that believeth; to the Jew first, and also to the Greek."* The power of God works through the gospel of Christ. Therefore, if I believe the gospel of Christ, the power of God should work in my life. If the power of God is not working in my life, then I must examine my version of the gospel.

In verse 17, Paul clued us in to his understanding of the gospel of Christ. *"For therein is the righteousness of God revealed from faith to faith: as it is written, The just shall live by faith."* The Gospel reveals righteousness *"from faith to faith,"* not faith to works.

Any message that does not reveal righteousness from faith to faith is not the Gospel (Good News) at all. The Good News about

Jesus is that He obtained righteousness by His faith, and we accept that righteousness with our faith. Nothing else is good news; it is just law and works rehashed.

Thus, in order to guard our hearts, we must, first and foremost, guard them in the area of our righteousness. We must not allow anything to creep into our belief systems that will bring us back under law for righteousness. This is the issue of the majority of the New Testament.

The moment I start trusting in my righteousness, according to Galatians 2:21, the grace of God is neutralized. It stops working. Christ stops being able to affect my life. I am limited to my own ability to live righteous. God's ability no longer has access to my heart.

This does not mean I will immediately fall into sin. Rather, it means I will conquer only the sins that I have the ability to conquer. It means I can live only as clean as *I have the ability*. It means that I will eventually grow weary from doing good deeds, and that I will become bitter when things don't work out as they should. (See Hebrews 12:15.) It means that if I get tired, angry, or weak in any way, I will fall.

Trusting in personal righteousness neutralizes faith.

If what you have works only when you try "really hard," it is not grace. If you succeed only when you have the ability, it is not grace. If you have protection just on the day you pray, then it is not grace. If your emotions change based on your performance, it is not grace.

If you are a strong person, you can live a pretty decent moral life without grace—but you will never enter into rest. You will never experience any more in this life than you have the ability to produce.

I know the frailty of my own ability. I can clearly remember where my ability got me. I don't want that again. Therefore, I guard my heart. I refuse to listen to anything that would move me away from my confidence in Jesus and cause me to put confidence in the flesh (my ability).

Be Careful What You Hear

We are told not only to avoid those calling themselves brothers while they are still living in sin, but also to avoid those having *"a form of godliness, but denying the power thereof"* (2 Tim. 3:5). We, like the disciples, are to avoid the leaven of the Pharisees. In 1 Corinthians 1:17, Paul warned that the wisdom of words makes the cross of Christ to be of no effect. There are those who believe in Jesus; they are saved and are on their way to heaven. They just do not believe God can do what the Bible says He can—in *their* lives. There are also those who have wise-sounding persuasion that turns the weak away from the faith. Proverbs commands, *"Cease, my son, to hear instruction that causeth to err from the words of knowledge"* (Prov. 19:27).

This is not a call for judgment or criticism but for protection. All you hear and see will try to capture your heart. The breastplate of righteousness says, "No! If it's not in the Bible and of faith (the finished work of Jesus), I won't hear it." It was input from a fellow Israelite that challenged the call of Moses. It was input from his brothers that tried to rob Joseph of his dream. It was input from his own family that tried to keep Jesus from being who and what the Scripture said about Him. It was input from one of His most devoted apostles that tried to keep Jesus from going to the Cross. Likewise, it will be input from well-meaning, good people that will try to make you think your righteousness depends on your performance.

As harsh as it may sound, the Bible says, *"Let God be true, but every man a liar"* (Rom. 3:4). No matter how sincere or reasonable any counsel may sound, if it refutes the promises of God, you cannot accept or entertain it. Regardless of how godly or stable the person may be who offers such counsel, reject the counsel. Just don't reject the person. *"Prove all things; hold fast that which is good"* (1 Thess. 5:21).

Raise the Shield of Faith

By wearing the breastplate of righteousness, we operate in the realm of protection instead of cure. We protect our hearts from becoming crooked. We prevent unbelief instead of having to come out of it.

When any fiery dart comes, we are told how to handle it and be confident of absolute victory. Ephesians 6:16 promises, *"Above all, taking the shield of faith, wherewith ye shall be able to quench all the fiery darts of the wicked."* When we understand faith righteousness, we develop an entirely new concept of walking in faith.

Guard your heart with the righteousness of Christ.

If you study the Bible, you will find that the New Testament actually teaches very little about *faith for things*. From Romans forward, nearly every mention of faith deals with identity or righteousness. To raise the shield of faith is to raise or bring forth your righteousness, which is of Jesus.

Regardless of the situation, when we begin to look at, acknowledge, confess, or bring to mind the fact that we are righteous, then the grace of God flows from our hearts and makes us able to live that righteousness.

Too often we raise the shield of faith in *our* righteousness, rather than relying on *Christ's* righteousness at work in us. We ask ourselves, "Have I prayed enough? Have I confessed long enough? Have I been good enough? Have I done anything wrong?" The list is endless. And we always find a flaw. But my confidence is in nothing less than Jesus' blood and righteousness, which is sufficient.

Raising the shield of faith is very simply the continual rejection of anything not based on the finished work of Jesus. Wearing the breastplate of righteousness is guarding the heart with the righteousness we have in Jesus.

CHAPTER ELEVEN

THE DOORWAY TO THE HEART

Eleven

The Doorway to the Heart

The first entrance to the heart from this world is through the natural senses. Each sense is very powerful: taste, touch, smell, hearing, and sight. We have what seem to be corresponding senses in the spirit realm. The problem is, however, that we are more aware of input from this world than we are from the spirit world.

It is this world's input that we spend years receiving in school, on the evening news, and from messages that deny the power of God. The influence of the temporal world in our lives goes far beyond what most people imagine.

The term *world* often speaks of the world's system, which is completely different from God's system. Most of us have spent a lifetime learning how to successfully function within the world's system.

When we are born again, we fail to renew our minds after God's Word. Instead we take the wisdom of the world's system and try to function in the kingdom of God. It doesn't work. Romans 8:6 points out, *"For to be carnally minded is death; but to be spiritually minded is life and peace."*

The carnal mind is a mind that is set on the flesh—specifically the ability of the flesh to make one righteous. In the world's way of thinking, it makes sense that we would become righteous by doing righteous deeds, but that is being carnally minded. That is a mind that understands things according to the flesh. The carnal mind can never grasp that a righteous lifestyle flows forth from a person who is righteous.

Every believer must renew his mind if he is ever to function successfully in the kingdom of God. We must see things the way God says they are, not the way we decide they are. Our perception of reality must be totally consistent with God's; otherwise, we will fall into the category of the carnally minded.

Internal Information Produces External Actions

There is a very definite process by which we establish information in our hearts. Once we have received any input, whether true or false, we usually begin to think on it. Once we begin to think on anything—particularly those things that produce emotions—it begins to affect our hearts. In Mark 4:24, Jesus shows us how information is able to affect our lives. *"And He said to them, Be careful what you are hearing. The measure [of thought and study] you give [to the truth you hear] will be the measure [of virtue and knowledge] that comes back to you—and more [besides] will be given to you who hear"* (AMP).

Your heart reveals what you are.

Simply hearing a truth may not affect your life; but when you begin to think or meditate on it, it will. As you meditate on truth, that truth begins to be revealed, expanded, and made alive to you. As you ponder what you hear, those thoughts begin to affect your emotions and ultimately find their way into your heart.

Proverbs 23:7 says, *"For as he thinketh in his heart, so is he."* This Scripture contains a wealth of information. First, it simply states what we have already seen. A man is what he is in his heart. One will rarely rise above the condition of his heart. If he does, those times will be short and inconsistent. Your heart affects your life more than anything else. That is the standard you will always return to, no matter what happens.

Most people have emotional standards, health standards, financial standards, weight standards, relationship standards—life standards—that have been established in their hearts throughout the years. No matter what good fortune or misfortune comes along, they will always end up back at the level of their hearts.

The word *"thinketh"* in Proverbs 23:7 comes from two words. One means to split open and the other means porter or gatekeeper.

What you think determines what you will become.

The idea is this: your thoughts are the doorkeeper of your heart. The doorkeeper decides what will get in and out of the door. If your thoughts are thoughts of fear, the doorkeeper of your heart will become fear. The doorkeeper will let in, and it will let out, only those things that reinforce fear. Those thoughts you dwell on are forming your heart to make it straight or crooked. Every minute of every day, what you think is determining what your life will become.

Thoughts are like a guidance system in a missile. Some visual guidance systems capture an image of their target, then follow that image until they reach the destination—which is destruction. Likewise, our thoughts create images that guide our lives. We will unconsciously gravitate toward the direction of our thoughts.

If you think thoughts of fear, unbelief, or self-abasement, you will develop a heart to live that kind of life. If you think thoughts of faith, confidence, and self-worth, you will develop a heart that can receive the grace of God to fulfill those thoughts.

Again, your thoughts are the doorkeeper of your heart, and thoughts will give entry only to those thoughts that are after their own kind. If you were to go on a trip and leave a guard at your door, you would certainly want someone who would be honest and dependable. An honest man would stop the destroyer. A dishonest man would yield. Likewise, your thoughts determine what will have entry into your heart.

In some areas, you may believe exactly what the Word says and have absolute victory in that area. However, in another area you may not believe the truth. Therefore, you do not have the grace (God's ability) to live that truth. Grace is not a generalized function; it is not one of those things that you either have or don't have. There may be areas of your life in which it is easy to trust God; there may be other areas where it is impossible for you to trust God. Again, it is all a matter of what you believe about your righteousness.

When a person is established in faith righteousness, he becomes more stable in every area of life. Second Peter 2:8 teaches that what we see and hear has the power to vex our souls. When people are vexed, they are emotionally consumed. Their thoughts tend to be totally captivated by a person or situation. They are so consumed with that situation that just thinking about it produces the associated emotions.

A person who is vexed by a fear can think of the thing he fears, and it will produce emotions that come forth as if the thing he feared was actually happening. A person who is consumed with a sexual sin can think of that sin or a particular person and immediately be aroused. Therefore, he becomes consumed and totally dominated by his emotions.

Decisions Are Based on Beliefs

The will is determined, among other things, by emotions. The will is a function of the soul. The soul seems to consist of the mind (thoughts), the emotions (feelings), and the will (the ability to make decisions).

If we begin to think we are unrighteous or unacceptable to God, we begin to have feelings of unrighteousness; ultimately, we make decisions out of those thoughts and emotions. If those thoughts ever get established in our hearts, we will never rise above them without a change of heart.

Proverbs 12:6 says, *"The words of the wicked are to lie in wait for blood: but the mouth of the upright shall deliver them."* Words have the potential to take our blood.

Not every word that you hear has the ability to take your blood—only the ones you think on. When you think on truth or lies to the extent that they begin to affect your emotions, they are controlling your life. If you focus on them long enough, they will become part of your belief system—and those beliefs become the primary factor in your victory or defeat.

Words have the power to kill or to heal.

The Bible speaks of thoughts and feelings that come from the mind as well as from the deeper level of the heart. The thoughts and feelings that come from the heart—which is the seat of your beliefs—come effortlessly and guide your life's direction. For this reason, we must believe the truth about the finished work of Jesus. Nothing affects your life more than what you believe about your righteousness.

If you believe God cannot change you or if you believe you cannot come out of your sins, your heart is crooked in that area. The condition of your heart will determine what will happen in your life. Where there is no righteousness, grace cannot bring life. But when a person believes that he is righteous, the grace (ability of God) to live righteous flows forth from his heart.

Our real struggle in life is in the area of believing, not doing. You can do and not believe, but you can't believe and not do. Our belief systems affect every area of our lives.

Bring Your Thoughts in Line with the Word

Second Corinthians 10:3 says, *"For though we walk in the flesh, we do not war after the flesh."* Although we live in a body of flesh, our means of fighting the battles of life should never be according to our natural power. In 2 Corinthians 10:5, this warfare is described as taking place in the mind: *"Casting down imaginations, and every high thing that exalteth itself against the knowledge of God, and bringing into captivity every thought to the obedience of Christ."*

Vain imaginations or reasonings rise up in us and try to steal God's promises from us. Rationalizations tell us why we are the way we are—not who and what God says we are. Thus, our struggle is not with the devil; our struggle is with our own minds. We don't believe in the finished work of Jesus. Our hearts are not straight (righteous).

All such imaginations are the product of a crooked heart, a heart that has been bent to line up with what others have said about us. We have cast aside the truth of God's Word and accepted the things we reason to be acceptable. Verse 4 tells us to pull down these strongholds with the mighty power of God, but these strongholds are not in the heavenly places. They are not demons. These strongholds are thoughts and imaginations that are not based on truth. The result of disobedience is disastrous. In God's Word, we read,

> But this thing commanded I them, saying, Obey my voice, and I will be your God, and ye shall be my people: and walk ye in all the ways that I have commanded you, that it may be well unto you. But they hearkened not, nor inclined their ear, but walked in the counsels and in the imagination of their evil heart, and went backward, and not forward. (Jer. 7:23–24)

Any imaginations that are not consistent with the Word will cause us to go backward. They will guide our lives into total destruction by alienating us from God's grace. Every thought that is not consistent with the revealed knowledge of God is a stronghold and must be cast down.

A thought is not cast down, however, by our screaming at it in the name of Jesus. Second Corinthians says to bring our thoughts captive to the obedience of Christ. How do you do that? Simple! Jesus conquered every sin; therefore, you don't have to try to conquer them. When the thought, "I am vulnerable," comes, the question is not my obedience. The question is Jesus' obedience.

Did Jesus conquer this sin when He rose from the dead? Yes! Am I in Jesus? Yes! Then I am righteous and free from sin. When I begin to acknowledge that Jesus conquered sin and gave me righteousness by His resurrection, then grace to live that righteousness begins to flow through my life. I am not trying to make those thoughts obey me. I am bringing those thoughts in line with what Jesus' obedience has already provided.

In reality, if Jesus is Lord of our lives, then we are obligated to believe only what God says about us. We have no right to believe or think anything that can't be substantiated by God's Word. When thoughts arise that do not line up with the promises of God, they must be dealt with immediately. Remember the shield of faith? *"Above all, taking the shield of faith, wherewith ye shall be able to quench all the fiery darts of the wicked"* (Eph. 6:16). The shield of faith will not quench some of the fiery darts; it will quench or extinguish *all* of them. Those fiery darts are the words, thoughts, or lusts that rise up to take your blood.

Go on the Offensive: Speak the Truth

Do not allow unrighteous thoughts to reside in your mind. Remember, any thought that does not line up with the finished work of Jesus is unrighteous. That unrighteousness will prevent God's grace from working in you. Always replace unscriptural thoughts with the promises of God. Settle every question about righteousness with the acknowledgment of Jesus' righteousness and the fact that you are in Him.

If your soul has been vexed, you cannot change your thoughts by simply trying to think on something else. The second half of Proverbs 12:6 says, *"The mouth of the upright* [righteous] *shall deliver them."* Paul said he boasted in his confident expectation of the view and opinion of God, which was reality. (See Romans 5:2.) This is how Paul prevailed in tribulation. This is also how you and I can prevail in the battle against sin, poor self-worth, and anything else that keeps us from walking in all that God says we can.

As I begin to verbally acknowledge my righteousness in Jesus, my every emotion begins to come in line with that truth. It is not something I am simply saying; it is a fact that I believe and that I feel. The truth is, you can't give in to sin when you feel righteous.

Conquering your thought life—more than any other single thing—will guard your heart against those things that rise up against the Word of God. When any thought or word tries to take your thoughts captive, you must raise the shield of faith. It is not enough to try to change what you think. When something has you vexed, you must speak God's truth out of your mouth. Proverbs 12:6 says, *"The mouth of the upright shall deliver them."* Boldly speak God's Word until your thoughts and emotions come back in line and you do not frustrate the grace of God.

Faith is believing and confessing.

It is said that it takes only weeks to establish a habit. Just think, it takes only six to eight weeks for anything to become natural. By consistently bringing your thoughts in line for a short time, you could totally transform your thinking habits. Six or eight weeks is a small price to pay for a lifetime of victory.

By habitually thinking thoughts that are consistent with God's Word, the doorway to your heart will allow only faith and grace to reign in your life.

CHAPTER TWELVE

COMING OUT OF THE GRAVE

Twelve

Coming Out of the Grave

W hat shall we say then? Shall we continue in sin, that grace may abound? God forbid. How shall we, that are dead to sin, live any longer therein?" (Rom. 6:1–2). As we discussed previously, grace is not God's ability to overlook sin. Rather, God is merciful to us when we sin. Because He is merciful, we can receive forgiveness, reconciliation, and grace (God's ability) to overcome sin. However, now that God has given us the ability to overcome sin, we are more obligated to deal with it. The true message of grace requires more responsibility on the part of every believer. Because of God's grace, we now have no excuse for sin.

We will deal with our sin only when we have removed every excuse for staying in it. Romans 6:14 says it plainly: *"For sin shall not be your master, because you are not under law, but under grace"* (NIV). That should be the end of all discussion. You will recall that righteousness demands that we see it God's way. So sin does not have any power over us now that we are in grace. When we were in the flesh, dependent on our power, sin reigned over us. But now we have the power of God. Sin has no place in our lives.

The Power That Works in Us

Now that we have accepted God's view, we have no excuse to stay in sin; we must deal with sin in a biblical way. Trying to conquer sin by works, mere will, or tenacity will be a very frustrating and self-righteous experience. We feel good about ourselves as long as we do good. We do good as long as we are able; but when we are no longer able, we will not do good. Then we will not feel good, and we will not have victory.

Grace brings responsibility.

Self-righteousness feels good about self only as long as self is doing righteous works. Faith righteousness feels good about self as long as self is in Christ.

In Ephesians 1, Paul prayed that we would have revelation knowledge about three particular things. One of the things he prayed is for us to understand *"the exceeding greatness of his power to us-ward who believe"* (Eph. 1:19). If we are to have victory, it is essential that we understand the power of God that works in our lives. Paul described this power to be

> *according to the working of his mighty power, which he wrought in Christ, when he raised him from the dead, and set him at his own right hand in heavenly places, far above all principality, and power, and might, and dominion, and every name that is named.* (Eph. 1:19–21)

The power that works in us is resurrection power. It is the same power that went into the grave to raise Jesus from the dead. It is the power that caused Him to be victorious over all other power.

Before coming to Jesus, we were dead in sin. We could not stop sinning, and we could not stop the results of sin. Jesus said in John 5:24, *"Verily, verily, I say unto you, He that heareth my word, and believeth on him that sent me, hath everlasting life, and shall not come into condemnation; but is passed from death unto life."* We were already dead; therefore, salvation is a resurrection from the dead.

The Bible teaches that Jesus became sin. If He died as a sinner and took the punishment that we deserve, then there is no doubt that He went to hell at death. Laden with the sins of the world, He was bound to the sinner's eternal destiny. All this was to deliver us from that penalty. Yet He did not remain in hell. The Scripture was fulfilled: *"Thou wilt not leave my soul in hell"* (Acts 2:27).

How did Jesus come out of the grave? When Jesus rose from the dead, He did not just conquer sin. He conquered sin and death. It is obvious that the resurrection gave Him victory over death, but what gave Him victory over sin?

Since Jesus died a sinner, it was the sins of the world that held Him in hell. So when the Spirit of God entered the bowels of the earth to come upon the Lord Jesus, He had to break the power of sin. Likewise, He had to break every demonic stronghold in the earth and in the heavens. As a result, all the sin of the world and all the forces of darkness could not keep Jesus from rising and ascending to the Father.

When Jesus came out of that grave, He not only conquered death; He also conquered sin. In actuality, Jesus didn't nail sins to the cross. According to Colossians 2:14, He nailed the law to the cross. That verse says, He *"blott*[ed] *out the handwriting of ordinances that was against us, which was contrary to us, and took it out of the way, nailing it to his cross."*

He nailed the law to the cross. He bore our sins to hell. The Old Testament type is seen in the scapegoat, which bore the sins of the people *outside the camp.* It was those sins that brought Him to the grave, but God raised Him from the dead. That same power that raised Jesus from the dead is the power that works in us. (See Ephesians 1:19–20.) It is that resurrection power that broke the sins of the entire world that works in you to break your individual sins, to raise you up into newness of life.

What Is Reality?

We did not get saved so that we could become righteous. We became righteous so that we could be saved. One of the greatest tragedies of salvation happens when a person is first born again: he is told only to believe on Jesus as his Savior. He does not know that Jesus is his righteousness. He does not know that He is giving him the power of righteousness.

Because of this ignorance, we are like the Galatians who started out by the Spirit, then tried to come to perfection by their own efforts (the flesh). *"Are ye so foolish? having begun in the Spirit, are ye now made perfect by the flesh?"* (Gal. 3:3).

We were not given the gift of righteousness so that we could live in sin. We were given righteousness so that we could be delivered from sin and its results. Therefore, Colossians 3:1 declares, *"If ye then be risen with Christ, seek those things which are above, where Christ sitteth on the right hand of God."*

Romans 6:4 says it was the glory of God that raised Jesus from the dead. Remember our previous discussion of glory? When we think of God's glory, we usually think of His radiance, splendor, and brightness. His glory is all that, but it is more. This word for *glory* means the view, judgment, and opinion of God, which is reality.

Righteousness delivers believers from sin.

The way God sees it is the way it is. Regardless of how we see it or understand it, God's view is reality.

Before Jesus ever was made flesh, before He ever walked the earth, before He ever went to the cross, and before He ever went to hell, God had spoken the reality. Men of old had prophesied about the cross and the judgment. It also had been spoken that Jesus was the Lord of Glory. He was the Savior of all men. He would be raised from the dead, and He would be a High Priest forever *"after the order of Melchizedek"* (Ps. 110:4). That was the reality. It did not look like reality when Jesus was on the cross. It did not look like reality when Jesus was in hell, but it was.

The Messianic Psalms and the book of Jonah describe the torment that went on while Jesus was in hell. Those passages show that

He confessed God's promises. The prophet Jonah confessed (as a type of Christ), *"The LORD...he heard me;...thou heardest my voice"* (Jonah 2:2); *"I will look again toward thy holy temple"* (v. 4); *"Thou brought up my life"* (v. 6); *"My prayer came in unto thee, into thine holy temple"* (v. 7); and *"I will sacrifice unto thee....Salvation is of the LORD"* (v. 9). These confessions of faith, worship, and trust were not made after Jonah was delivered. They were made from the whale's belly, which was a type of Jesus in hell. Jesus began to say, in hell, what God said. He began to worshipfully speak God's view and opinion, which is reality. Those words brought the Holy Spirit in and delivered Him from the chains of sin and death to make Him the firstborn from the dead.

This is why Paul could say in Romans 5:3, *"And not only so, but we glory in tribulations also."* That particular word for *"glory"* means joyful boast. Paul said in the previous verses that he joyfully boasted in the glory (view and opinion) of God. Even in tribulation, he boasted in God's view and opinion. Why? Because that is reality.

Confess the Reality—God's View of You

No matter what you are struggling with, God's reality is that you have victory. You are righteous. You are an overcomer. But if you don't believe God's view and opinion, grace cannot come forth and make you able to live in God's reality.

When we go through tribulation, our hearts can be affected. We receive negative, contrary information from many external sources. Our emotions might begin to change and our hearts begin to waver, but we can stabilize our hearts by what we say.

Even Jesus was nearly overcome by His emotions when He was in hell. Jonah, as a type of Jesus, said, *"The waters compassed me about, even to the soul: the depth closed me round about, the weeds were wrapped about my head"* (Jonah 2:5). He was describing an extremely emotional situation.

Then in Jonah 2:7, we see the ultimate struggle. *"When my soul fainted within me I remembered the LORD: and my prayer came in unto thee, into thine holy temple."* Although all Jesus' emotions were being swayed, He remembered the Lord God. Likewise, we must remember our Lord God. We must remember and acknowledge what He has done, and we must completely believe in, rely on, and acknowledge that finished work.

To be swayed by emotions, to make decisions from our perspective, is to observe a lying vanity. Jonah 2:8 notes, *"They that observe lying vanities forsake their own mercy."* Unfortunately, we tend to observe lying vanities—our views and opinions—with no real regard or trust for the view and opinion of God.

Trust in Christ's finished work.

As we acknowledge what God says, our hearts become persuaded and grace flows forth. Our emotions remain stable. We keep the doorkeeper of truth. We maintain the breastplate of righteousness. We maintain a heart that the Holy Spirit can work in and through.

We were born again by believing and confessing Jesus as the resurrected Lord of our lives. (See Romans 10:10.) But we continue to come forth out of those things that try to hold us in the grave of sin the same way. As we worshipfully confess what God says about us, the Spirit of glory and grace raises us from those things that try to claim lordship over us. The same Spirit that set Christ at the right hand of the Father seats us in *"heavenly places, far above all principality, and power, and might, and dominion"* (Eph. 1:20–21), to partake of the resurrected life.

CHAPTER THIRTEEN

THE TIME OF NEED

Thirteen

The Time of Need

We all have had certain situations in which we wondered if we would endure. I have seen people make great sacrifices at such times. With admiration, I have wondered if I could make that same sacrifice—with joy. But because of fear of certain situations, some people avoid specific types of ministry; consequently, they may miss the call of God. Sadly, even the fear of failure has kept many believers from having fruitful lives.

We often live in fear of certain temptations. We may have areas in which we have repeatedly failed. We lose all confidence in ourselves and in God's ability to deliver us in those particular areas. As a result, the fear of a certain sin keeps us from even trying to deal with it. We remain bound and crippled by that fear.

One of the things I've noticed about the grace of God is that it comes only at the point of need. Another thing I have seen is that when grace is working in us, we always have peace and joy. I have endured many difficult situations with unbelievable peace and joy. When I looked back, I would think, How did I endure that? I knew that I could not go through it again. Then I realized that it was God's strength that had brought me through.

Several years ago while working in street ministry, I had my life threatened many times. More than once, people came to my house for the purpose of attacking and possibly killing me. Although fear tried to dominate me, I was amazed by the strength that came into me. Once a man threw me across the hood of my car. He even had a gun in my face, but the peace of God was all over me. That is not my normal response. But in the time of need, God can deliver us from our normal and natural abilities.

Not Until You Need It

Time after time, God has given me the ability to endure very difficult situations with great joy, but the grace never came until the need was there. When I began going out on the streets to witness, I always dreaded it. I knew God wanted me to go, but I did not want to face the rejection. Often I would drive around and around the block. I dreaded the very thought of getting out. I made every imaginable excuse for not witnessing to anyone. However, as I prayed and "went," grace began to work in me. Within a few minutes, I was powerfully witnessing with great joy. The grace never came while I was waiting; it always came as I was going.

The Bible says, *"Faith without works is dead"* (James 2:20). If I had continued sitting in my car, praying and waiting on the Lord to give me strength, it probably would not have come. But because I prayed in faith and expectancy, I then began to take steps. First, I would park the car—still no strength. Then I would get out of the car—still no strength. Then I would walk the streets, reluctantly looking for someone to whom to witness—still no strength. Then I would spot a target—still no strength. But when I opened my mouth, God's strength came. The grace, strength, and ability of God came at the time of need. Real faith took hold of grace.

Strength is given in your time of need.

The Bible tells us to *"come boldly unto the throne of grace, that we may obtain mercy, and find grace to help in time of need"* (Heb.

4:16). You do not get the strength until there is a need. This is a key to walking in victory. Often the fear of a situation is worse than the situation itself. In Psalm 64:1, David prayed, *"Hear my voice, O God, in my prayer: preserve my life from fear of the enemy."* It was fear that was defeating him, not the enemy. Fear paralyzes our emotions. When fear comes, all our strength floods out of our bodies. First John 4:18 accurately states that *"fear hath torment."* However, we must realize when the time of need arises that we can receive grace to conquer.

We do not need the grace *now;* we need it in the *"time of need."* Our greatest times of need are not going to be in times of ministry. Our greatest times of need will always be in day-to-day life. The battles to conquer attitudes and temptations will be the greatest needs we ever have for grace.

Claim Your Righteousness in Christ

The Bible says to confidently approach God's throne during our times of need. In the area of temptation, our greatest times of need are when we are about to sin or when we have already sinned. These are the times that we should have the least amount of boldness and the greatest amount of need.

If I am being drawn into sin, I must know that God still accepts me. Otherwise I will not run to Him to receive mercy and grace to help in my time of need. Out of fear and guilt, I will run from the One who is able to deliver me from sin.

Likewise, if I have given in to a sin, I will never find God's ability to get out of that sin if I cannot go to Him in confidence. The only thing that can produce that kind of confidence is righteousness. If I am righteous, I am free to go to God at any stage of the temptation and receive the grace I need.

This concept is totally unacceptable to the carnal mind. How can we call ourselves righteous if we have sinned? Well, the Corinthian church was known as the most carnal church in the New Testament. Yet they were the very people to whom Paul said, "You are the righteousness of God in Christ." (See 2 Corinthians 5:21.)

If I deny my righteousness, I have not denied me; I have denied Christ. Now, confessing your righteousness is not easy to do. When everything in your emotions is telling you how unrighteous you are, it is not easy to stand there and acknowledge your righteousness. Yet that is the only thing that will bring forth grace. When righteousness is truly established in your heart, that will be the end of your sin problem.

You can put an end to your "sin problem."

Hebrews 4:16 says to *"come boldly unto the throne of grace."* We may not have boldness in conquering our sins. We may not have boldness in any of our abilities, but we can have boldness and confidence in God. All we need to know when approaching the throne of grace is the total acceptance of God. This acceptance does not change us, but it places us in an environment conducive to change. If we do not believe God's acceptance, we will never receive His grace.

You Must Decide

One thing God will never do is to violate your will. He will convict you, draw you, and compel you, but He will not change your mind for you. God requires us to repent. The word *repent* means to have a change of mind. We are required to have a change of mind. Only after we have repented, changed our minds, and made a decision will God move in our lives.

So many people look at a particular sin that has them bound—one that they have fallen into repeatedly—and they lose their confidence to the point that they are afraid to trust God. You ask them to make a decision, but they will not. Why? They have failed so many times that they are afraid to step out again. Most people's attitude about change of any kind is, "If I could, I would try to change." The problem is that people are waiting until they *feel* they are able before they will commit to anything. However, grace works just the opposite. The truth is, If they would try to change, they could.

We have to will to do something before the grace of God can make us able. We are not robots; we have a will. Until we repent, until we change our minds, we limit what God can do.

I have learned that my job is to decide (repent) and trust God to make me able. It is then God's job to empower me. Isaiah said, *"If ye be willing and obedient, ye shall eat the good of the land"* (Isa. 1:19). Most people understand the need for obedience, but few understand the need for willingness.

In most cases of failure, a clear-cut decision was never made. Those individuals decided to "try" to change. They wanted something to happen, but they never decided, "I have victory over this thing now." Most people are afraid to make those kinds of decisions, yet that is precisely what it takes to get the job done.

The reason we are not willing to commit to absolute victory is because we base our believing on our own track records. We try to bring everything captive to our level of obedience instead of to Jesus' level of obedience.

If my level of obedience was all that great, I would not need Jesus. I would not have any problems. The fact that I need to make changes, the fact that I have problems, tells me I can have little or no confidence in my abilities. However, I can make an absolutely confident decision about victory in any area if I base it on the finished work of Jesus. I do not need to fear the limitations of His ability.

When we repent, God empowers.

On the practical side, I also have learned that change that does not come immediately is no reflection of whether change will come.

There have been some areas where I have made absolute decisions and commitments to change, and those changes were slow in coming. Why? God had to work in my heart to bring about those changes. But I am no longer afraid to decide.

Don't "Try"; Decide

Remember, faith righteousness takes hold of grace. (See Ephesians 2:8.) We must use our faith righteousness to access the grace we need for every situation. Faith believes and confesses the Word of God, which brings the grace for salvation. (See Romans 10:10.) Faith makes a positive, present-tense confession and decision. Faith does not believe God is going to; faith believes God has. Faith knows that the work of the Cross is complete; therefore, it is all available to us now.

When you were born again, it did not happen because you decided to give God a try. If you are like me, you "tried" several times before you made a real decision. You see, I was afraid to make an absolute decision. I was afraid I could not do it. So I gave it a try. I was right; I could not do it. I did not have the strength to live for God.

One day I made a decision. I believed the truth, I made a firm confession of my commitment to Jesus, and I was able. I did not understand what took place at the time, but I know now. Faith makes an absolute decision, and it takes faith to get grace. Job 22:28 says, *"You shall also decide and decree a thing, and it shall be established"* (AMP).

Sin is rooted in self-centeredness. Because a certain sin gratifies our desires, we give into it, not because we have to, but because we want to. Most of us say, "God, make me not want this anymore." For most people that will never happen, not because God is unwilling or unable, but because we do not make absolute decisions. God can change your desires only after there has been real repentance. If you have not decided, you have not repented.

There are some simple reasons why we don't decide about sin. Few people see sin as the source of their pain. They think their pain is God's conviction, but they are wrong. Every pain in our lives is linked to a sinful belief or behavior. Yet we don't see and believe that.

I recently asked my congregation this simple question: "When you got saved, did you stop sinning because it was the right thing to do? Because you had to? Or because you wanted to?" Many people quit sinning only because they have to. Those people will never be able to make quality decisions (repent) about sin.

Sin is the source of pain.
We view sin as that long list of fun things that God does not allow us to do, while we view serving God as that long list of difficult things we must do. We even have clichés that say, "This is so good that it must be sinful. We had so much fun that it must have been sin." These statements reflect our attitudes toward sin.

God wants you out of sin for a reason: He does not want you to be destroyed by its power. He does not want sin to affect your ability to have a meaningful relationship with Him or with those around you.

Until we see sin as a list of things that bring absolute destruction, we will cling to it and make excuses for it. We will find every reason—theological, emotional, or otherwise—to justify staying in sin. But the real truth is that we can come out of sin when we want to. Because of grace, no sin has dominion over us!

If you want God's grace, then you must make a firm decision, confess the Word of God, and start taking steps. When the grace of God comes, there will be victory with joy. Victory over sin is not quitting sin but still wanting to give in to it; real victory comes when we see the utter pain and destruction of sin in our lives, make an absolute decision about sin and victory, and trust victory to happen because of God's power in us.

CHAPTER FOURTEEN

FREED FROM SIN

Fourteen

Freed from Sin

The Holy Spirit is identified by several names. Each of these names reflects a certain aspect of His nature and work in the life of the believer. In Hebrews 10:29, He is referred to as the *"Spirit of grace."* This name identifies Him as the One who works in us to make us able.

Understanding that grace is God's ability opens our understanding to the new covenant. It is the very issue of grace that so radically separates the new covenant from the Old.

To define grace simply as unmerited favor forever maintains the veil that darkens our understanding. All that the Old Testament believers had was unmerited favor. As people who were not born again, as people who did not have the righteousness of God, all they could hope for was unmerited favor. But, according to Scripture, their actions never made them righteous enough to receive God's favor. *"Therefore by the deeds of the law there shall no flesh be justified in his sight: for by the law is the knowledge of sin"* (Rom. 3:20).

Remember, the weakness of the law was the flesh. *"For what the law could not do, in that it was weak through the flesh, God sending his own Son in the likeness of sinful flesh, and for sin, condemned sin in the flesh"* (Rom. 8:3).

As I have said before, flesh is man's ability. A man in the flesh is a man who is attempting to be made righteous by his own ability.

We are *"in the Spirit"* (Rom. 8:9) when we walk *"after the Spirit"* (v. 4) for our ability to have righteousness. *"That the righteousness of the law might be fulfilled in us, who walk not after the flesh, but after the Spirit"* (v. 4). Therefore, God has freely given the Spirit of grace to us to make us able to live a powerful, godly, victorious life. As the Spirit of grace, He continually works in us to make us able to conquer sin. He is the "One called alongside to help." As the Helper, He gives us the ability to do those things we decide to do. It is up to us to believe and decide to come out of sin; He is here to help by giving us the ability.

Sin Is a Choice

A failure to understand grace has probably kept more people bound to sin than anything else. Defining grace as nothing more than unmerited favor lends itself to saying that "God can still give me favor when I sin." We have a doctrine of grace that says sin is wrong, but God winks at my sin. How contradictory!

The truth about grace actually says, "I don't have to sin. Sin has no power over me. I am not limited to my ability to deal with sin. Yes, God will continue to love me and accept me if I sin, but that is an issue of mercy, not grace."

I am so thankful for God's love, mercy, and forgiveness when I sin. However, I am even more thankful for His grace that delivers me from having to yield to sin.

In light of this truth, sin under the new covenant is much more serious than sin under the old covenant. Because we have been delivered from sin, all sin is willful. It may be done in ignorance or unknowingly, but it is always done as an act of the will. A saved person always sins by choice. We all try to convince ourselves otherwise, but sin does not have dominion over us; to sin is always a choice.

Born-again Christians are free from the power of sin. We may choose not to believe that and thereby yield to sin, but, regardless of our views and opinions, that does not change God's view and opinion. Romans 6:14 states, *"For sin shall not have dominion over you: for ye are not under the law, but under grace."*

Grace removes the excuse to sin.

An amazing thing about sin is not only that it is willful, but also that we choose our sins. We give in only to the sins that we enjoy. No one gives in to the sins that he hates. People may hate the results, they may hate getting caught, but they do not hate their sin.

As severe as this is, we must realize the truth about it. We cannot use grace as an excuse to sin. Let us realistically accept the responsibility of our actions. God is merciful and forgiving. We do not need to enter into fear, but we must accept responsibility. Fear will only keep us from properly dealing with sin.

Taking Responsibility

The paradox of the grace message is responsibility. Many people accused Paul of encouraging sin because he rejected law and preached grace, but actually the very opposite was true. The law provides all kinds of excuses for sin.

Grace, on the other hand, strips us of every excuse. The person in the new covenant who yields to sin can only admit to unbelief or choice—both of which can be reduced to personal responsibility. Nothing scares a person more than responsibility. Personal responsibility, however, is the only pathway to freedom. Personal responsibility says, "I must believe God and depend on the Holy Spirit to make this work."

The natural-minded (carnal) person cannot relate to the real issues of faith (faith righteousness). The carnal-minded person cannot accept righteousness as a free gift because he sees righteousness as a work of the flesh. The following Scriptures explain the dilemma of the person who sees righteousness as an effort of the flesh:

> *For they that are after the flesh do mind the things of the flesh; but they that are after the Spirit the things of the Spirit....Because the carnal mind is enmity against God: for it is not subject to the law of God, neither indeed can be. So then they that are in the flesh cannot please God.* (Rom. 8:5, 7–8)

The Holy Spirit is grieved when we refuse to believe that we are righteous and choose not to walk in that righteousness.

> *Neither yield ye your members as instruments of unrighteousness unto sin: but yield yourselves unto God, as those that are alive from the dead, and your members as instruments of righteousness unto God.* (Rom. 6:13)

But if you don't believe you can yield yourself to God, you will not make a decision to yield. Failure to make a decision limits what the Spirit of grace can do in your life.

Avoid Torment—Choose Wisely

If you yield to sin, sin will rule your life—even though you have been given the power to overcome sin. If you yield to righteousness, the Holy Spirit will give you the grace to walk in that righteousness. But the choice is yours.

This responsibility becomes a source of mental torment for the believer. Romans 8:1 says, *"There is therefore now no condemnation to them which are in Christ Jesus, who walk not after the flesh, but after the Spirit."* According to Thayer's Greek-English lexicon, the *word "condemnation"* means a damnatory sentence. The believer who tries to walk in the flesh (human ability) for righteousness lives in mental torment because there is a constant expectation of judgment.

The mental torment of sin is horrendous. Hebrews 10:26–27 describes the plight of the new covenant believer who yields to sin.

> *For if we sin wilfully after that we have received the knowledge of the truth, there remaineth no more sacrifice for sins, but a certain fearful looking for of judgment and fiery indignation, which shall devour the adversaries.*

The attempt to walk in righteousness by the flesh brings torment and makes us vulnerable to sin. Then when we do sin, there is another type of torment. The very reason we yielded to sin is found in Hebrews 10:29:

> *Of how much sorer punishment, suppose ye, shall he be thought worthy, who hath trodden under foot the Son of God, and hath counted the blood of the covenant, wherewith he was sanctified, an unholy thing, and hath done despite unto the Spirit of grace?*

Yielding to sin, supposing oneself to be under the dominion of sin, is tantamount to denying everything that the new covenant and the Spirit of grace make available for us.

Usually after we sin, condemnation creeps in, and we fall into a world of shame and despair. We look for and expect judgment. We are tormented with fear. It is amazing how the devil convinces us that we will enjoy sin. He makes us sure God will forgive us. Then, when we give in, he tells us how dirty we are and how God could not possibly love someone like us.

Sin will rule your life if you yield to it.

Have you fallen? The Bible has great news for you! *"For a just* [righteous] *man falleth seven times, and riseth up again"* (Prov. 24:16). Being righteous does not mean one never falls; it means he gets up when he falls! If one is righteous in his heart, he knows that he cannot continue in sin. The Holy Spirit continually reminds him of his righteousness. Every sin that he commits is contrary to his righteous nature. Thus, there comes a time when the believer can no longer deny his righteous nature; he has to get up.

The pain of sin is not the Holy Spirit making us miserable. Our consciences make us miserable. The Holy Spirit convicts the *"world of sin, and of righteousness, and of judgment"* (John 16:8). We are not the world. We are His disciples, and He leads us into the truth.

When we are faced with truth, our consciences condemn us. Condemnation is never a work of the Spirit. The Spirit is continually trying to make you see the truth about you in Jesus. The Holy Spirit is always telling you that you are righteous, that you are an overcomer and can make it. He is trying to draw you back into fellowship with the Father.

What Happens When We Sin?

First John, though often used to tell sinners how to get saved, is not written to sinners. It is written to Christians who sin. First John 1:5 says, *"God is light, and in him is no darkness at all."* Light, in the Scripture, is synonymous with truth and life. Light also suggests the absence of deceit. God deals in truth, righteousness, and honesty.

The passage continues to say, *"If we say that we have fellowship with him, and walk in darkness, we lie, and do not the truth"* (v. 6). When we walk in any darkness (untruth, unrighteousness, sin, deceit), we are no longer in fellowship with God. I believe there has been much misunderstanding about this verse. Many people say that your sin will separate you from God. That is totally untrue under the new covenant. The new covenant says nothing shall separate us from the love of God. Paul wrote, *"Nor height, nor depth, nor any other creature, shall be able to separate us from the love of God, which is in Christ Jesus our Lord"* (Rom. 8:39).

Even the withdrawal of fellowship is on our part. God does not draw back; we are the ones who draw back.

Departing from truth frustrates God's grace.

Colossians 1:21 says, *"And you, that were sometime alienated and enemies in your mind by wicked works, yet now hath he reconciled."* Alienation from God is a product of wicked works, but only in our minds.

When we sin, our hearts (consciences) condemn us. But God is greater than our hearts. *"For if our heart condemn us, God is greater than our heart, and knoweth all things"* (1 John 3:20). In other words, God does not change, but in our hearts, we change.

Guilt will not bring repentance (change of mind). Guilt will bring fear and a withdrawal of fellowship. Guilt assumes that the other person involved is against us.

I had several thousands of dollars in bad checks that were given to me in one of my businesses. Every one of those people who wrote me a bad check once considered me a real friend. I did nothing to prosecute or harass them; I offered only a willingness to work out terms.

Nevertheless, those people, to whom I extended kindness, have found all kinds of fault with me. Why? When there is guilt, there is a need for alleviation of that guilt. The most natural way to justify guilt is to find fault with the one you think is the source of your pain. When you think anyone is bringing you pain, that person becomes your enemy.

We react in the same way in our relationship with God. We assume that He is the source of our pain. Because of our faulty belief systems, we believe that He is angry with us. We assume that we are enemies, so we withdraw from fellowship with Him. All these thoughts, which are being taught in churches across America, are darkness. They are untruth, unrighteousness, deceit, and vain imaginations. Yet because we believe them, we are alienated from God in our minds.

When we depart from the truth, God's grace does not work in our lives. We can experience His grace only when we believe the truth. Remember, grace works through righteousness. Departing from truth frustrates the grace of God. (See Galatians 2:21.) The word *frustrate,* according to Thayer's Greek-English lexicon, means to nullify or make void. In other words, when we depart from Bible truth, we make void the power and ability of God. *"But if we walk in the light, as he is in the light, we have fellowship one with another, and the blood of Jesus Christ his Son cleanseth us from all sin"* (1 John 1:7). Walking in the light will get us out of sin, but trying to come out of sin to get God's love and approval is darkness. It is a rejection of all that the new covenant came to give us.

The main area of light we need to walk in is our righteousness. The carnal mind says, "You can't be righteous; you sinned." But a mind of the Spirit says, "Yes, I have sinned, but I repent of that sin. Sin is wrong, but I am still righteous in Jesus. I am not a slave to this sin. Jesus conquered this sin when He arose from the dead. God loves and accepts me. I don't have to be angry with God. God is not the source of my pain. Sin is the source of my pain." This kind of believing will allow grace to flow freely.

Walking in the Light

First John 1:7 says *"But if we walk in the light, as he is in the light, we have fellowship one with another."* That phrase, *"fellowship with one another"* does not mean believers are in fellowship; it speaks of believers fellowshiping with God. Acknowledging the truth sets us free to run *to* God, instead of running *from* Him. It frees us from the destruction of shame and disgrace. The prophet Isaiah spoke of this day:

> *For your shame ye shall have double; and for confusion they shall rejoice in their portion: therefore in their land they shall possess the double: everlasting joy shall be unto them.*
>
> (Isa. 61:7)

The last half of 1 John 1:7 is essential: *"And the blood of Jesus Christ his Son cleanseth us from all sin."* You are already cleansed from sin; the truth is you are clean from sin. Your spirit man is as clean and as perfect as it will ever be. There is nothing you can add to what Jesus has done in your spirit. At the same time, your soul and your heart are affected by sin. When you sin, it damages your confidence in God. It damages your confidence in the Word of God. It destroys your hope of newness of life.

Lenski in *The Interpretation of St. Paul's Epistle to the Romans* notes that *"all sin"* refers to more than just the sins committed; it actually refers to the sin principle or the root of the sin. Since we have been born again, our sins do not have their root in the sin nature; we no longer have that nature. Instead, they have their root in our belief systems and in our emotions.

First John 1:9 is crucial to walking out the victory that Jesus gives. *"If we confess our sins, he is faithful and just to forgive us our sins, and to cleanse us from all unrighteousness."* First, we must recognize the need to confess sin. Confessing sin is not confessing that you are a sinner. You are not a sinner; you are a saint made righteous by the blood of Jesus.

The word *confess* literally means to say the same thing. This is significant to walking in the light. When I say the same thing about my sin that God says, I must say that I am free from sin. I must say that sin has no dominion over me. I must say that I have a righteous nature. I also must say that forgiveness is mine through the finished work of Jesus.

Legally all sins have been forgiven, but that is not true experientially. Legally all men's sins have been paid for. All men's salvation has been purchased, yet not all men have experienced that salvation and forgiveness. It is only when men believe the truth about the Lord Jesus that righteousness comes into their hearts. It is when they confess this truth that they experience salvation.

Likewise, all believer's sins have been dealt with at the Cross. However, that truth will not affect your life if you do not believe and confess it. So confessing, saying the same thing God says about you and your sin, is the way you return to the light. It is in believing these truths that your heart becomes established in righteousness. It is in confessing these truths that you experience forgiveness.

Acknowledge what God says about your sin.

In light of this new covenant truth, I have not confessed my sin until I say the same thing about it that God says. As long as I have an excuse, I have not confessed. As long as I have someone to blame, I have not confessed. Not until I say, "I am righteous; I am free from the dominion of sin; I did this because I wanted to," not until then am I really confessing. A part of my confession also acknowledges God's forgiveness and mercy. A true confession acknowledges that God loves me and accepts me, no matter what my heart says. This is not "easy believism"; this is personal responsibility at its utmost.

If God loves, accepts, and forgives me, then I do not have the right to give in to depression over my sin. I do not have the right to walk around wondering if God hears my prayers.

Sometimes when my children were growing up, they would sneak off and do something they knew I would not approve of. What they did not know was that I already knew what they had done. Although their rebellion hurt and disappointed me, I still loved them and wanted fellowship with them. In my heart, I had already forgiven them.

After days or weeks of feeling guilty, they would finally come to me and tell the truth about what they had done. It would be at this point that they would experience the forgiveness that I had already given them. All of their avoiding me—avoiding eye contact, avoiding fellowship—was a product of the guilt in their own hearts. It was not "the same thing" that I was saying in my heart, but they could not experience my love and mercy until they came to me and believed me when I told them I had forgiven them.

We go through the same thing with God. He has already dealt with our sin at the Cross, yet we experience that mercy only when we confess our sins.

Go to the Root

Forgiveness deals with the fruit of the sin we commit; cleansing deals with the root of the sin. The reason we repeatedly fall into sins is a root problem. Sinning, receiving forgiveness, and going on our way is like picking fruit from a tree. Those apples or pears or peaches will grow back every year. You can spend the rest of your life in frustration, picking the same fruit year after year, or you can go to the root.

Our deepest need is a relationship with our Father. Man was created for that purpose. God so deeply wanted fellowship that He said, "I'll take care of the judgment for sin in One Man, instead of individual men. I will take care of separation from Me because of sin in One Man, instead of individual men. I also will give righteousness through One Man's efforts, instead of every man individually obtaining righteousness." With sin and righteousness taken care of, we can now have a relationship with God.

However, because we do not believe and walk in the light of Jesus' finished work, we do not have much fellowship with God. In that case, salvation becomes fire insurance. Prayer and Bible reading become premiums that we pay in order to keep the policy current. We end up so busy trying to pay the premiums that we do not have time for a relationship with the Father.

It is in intimate fellowship with God that He is able to purge my conscience from the effects of sin. His Word says, *"How much more shall the blood of Christ, who through the eternal Spirit offered himself without spot to God, purge your conscience from dead works to serve the living God?"* (Heb. 9:14). Dead works are all those religious works we do to earn a relationship with the Father. Yet, it is in fellowship and intimacy that I am freed from that "works righteousness" mentality.

Intimacy with God will annihilate sin's root.

It is also in close fellowship with Him that God brings healing to my heart and sets me free from those areas of selfishness, fear, and unbelief that cause me to yield to sin. Confession of what Jesus has done at the Cross brings the experience of forgiveness that gives me the courage to fellowship with God. Then I walk in the light of that reality by entering into fellowship with Him. In that time of intimacy, I am changed emotionally.

Through personal fellowship with the Father, you can experience the love and acceptance that will annihilate the root cause of the sin to which you have continually yielded. That sin does not have power over you. Your needs can be resolved only in a close, personal relationship with God.

FRUSTRATING THE GRACE OF GOD

Fifteen

Frustrating the Grace of God

We can experience grace at different levels, at different stages, and in many different ways. That is why Peter called it *"the manifold grace of God"* (1 Pet. 4:10). Of all the ways to experience grace, the greatest is continually. It has only one requirement—that our hearts be 100 percent persuaded that we are righteous and committed to walking in that righteousness.

A person whose heart is established in the Gospel really has very little to deal with in the area of sin and temptation. Jesus lived a life above sin because of the grace of God. John 1:14 shows the role grace played in the life of Jesus: *"And the Word was made flesh, and dwelt among us, (and we beheld his glory, the glory as of the only begotten of the Father,) full of grace and truth."* It was His belief about the truth that made grace effective in His life.

As your heart becomes more established in the truth of the Gospel, you will spend less time struggling and battling with sin and more time in fellowship with the Father. The Christian life will become "easy and light." (See Matthew 12:30.) Any message that makes it increasingly more difficult is not consistent with what Jesus promised.

Then, of course, there is grace that works in us when we face temptations or difficult situations. This is the grace most active in the life of the person who has not yet fully accepted righteousness through the Lord Jesus. When facing difficult situations, he will persuade his heart by the Word of God that he can do whatever the Word says. The confidence that comes by persuading his heart allows grace to flow forth. However, this is a rather inconsistent walk.

Qualified before God

In every situation, I have learned that *"I can do all things through Christ which strengtheneth me"* (Phil. 4:13). Because I know I am righteous, I never wonder if I am qualified for God to work on my behalf. I know that my qualification for God to work in me is the finished work of Jesus. Colossians 1:12 says, *"Giving thanks unto the Father, which hath made us meet* [qualified us] *to be partakers of the inheritance of the saints in light."* God has qualified me in Jesus.

Sometimes it is more difficult to appropriate grace when facing temptation. Why? Temptation is a breeding ground for condemnation. In order to understand the condemnation that comes with temptation, first one must understand its source. Temptation does not originate with the devil; it originates with us. *"But every man is tempted, when he is drawn away of his own lust, and enticed"* (James 1:14).

The word *lust* simply means desire. It does not necessarily mean an evil desire, just desire. Whether we desire something that is sinful or something that is godly, it is our trust in God and our confidence in our qualification that determines where we will turn for fulfillment.

If we believe all the promises to be ours, and if we believe that we are qualified, then we will turn trustingly to God and His Word. We will wait with patience for the Father to bring those promises into reality. There will be no fear, wondering, or wavering.

If, on the other hand, we feel that we must do something to qualify ourselves, we will lack the necessary confidence to receive from God. We will enter into dead works to try to convince God to do things for us.

The Temptation of the World's System

Second Peter 1:4 gives us insight into escaping the corruption that is in the world. These promises cause us to escape the corruption of the world:

Whereby are given unto us exceeding great and precious promises: that by these ye might be partakers of the divine nature, having escaped the corruption that is in the world through lust.

As I have mentioned before, the term *world* usually refers to the world's system. When we turn to the world's system, the world's view, the world's way of success, we have turned away from God and His Word. So the corruption that is in the world corrupts us when we try to obtain God's promises by working the world's system, a religious system, or any system other than trusting God.

Believe God's promises are for you.

Remember, however, that a major part of trust is trusting that we are qualified. It is not enough to believe that there are promises; we must believe that those promises are for us. We must accept the one and only qualifying factor for those promises—being in Christ Jesus!

Peter also pointed out that corruption is there through lust. It doesn't have to be lust for evil things; it can simply be lust (desire) for anything. It is not desiring things that makes lust turn into sin. It is the desire to have those things apart from God's Word as the system for receiving them that turns it into sin.

Many people who are called of God turn from God and try to fulfill their calls through the world's system. Because they do not really trust God, they seek to make His promises come to pass by using their own plans and schemes. This is just as wicked as any kind of sin. All unbelief is wicked. Unbelief either denies that God has given us the promise, or it denies that Jesus alone qualifies us to receive the promise.

The thing that makes temptation so condemning is that we want the thing we are being tempted to do. If we didn't want (desire, lust for) it, there would be no temptation. Usually we feel so condemned for wanting something that we assume God is displeased with us and will not help us. Therefore, since we are not **Which system are you trusting in— the world's or God's?** able to overcome the temptation using our own abilities, we fall.

It is important to understand this key issue about desire. Every desire you have is God-given. Satan cannot give you desire. The desire for sexual fulfillment is a God-given desire of the body. The desire to succeed is a God-given emotional need that is built into the human emotional makeup. All basic desires are God-given.

What God did not give us were the perverted methods people are willing to pursue in order to fulfill these desires. In a temptation, we are simply offered perverted ways of fulfilling our God-given desires. We yield to those desires because we do not believe that God's method of fulfillment is really the best.

We pervert godly sexual desires because we do not believe that a monogamous relationship with a person can give us the fulfillment that comes from sexual deviation. We are willing to use and abuse people to fulfill our dreams because we don't believe we can help others and still reach our goals. We trust the world's system more than we trust God's system.

Stay with Grace

Once we have sinned, we face the greatest religious temptation: to abandon grace. When a Christian falls, he feels that, in order to be restored, he must go back to doing what he was doing before. I beg to differ. If what you were doing before worked, you would not be where you are now! Nevertheless, our works mentality always focuses on *doing* rather than on *believing.*

When we go for counseling, we are told what we must start to do in order to get right with God. All this sounds very reasonable to the carnal mind. It makes sense. However, the key to restoration is the same as the key to victory—believing!

Trying to do things to be right is what got us into trouble to start with. Trying to be righteous in our own strength isolates us from grace. Paul said in Galatians 2:21, *"I do not frustrate the grace of God: for if righteousness come by the law, then Christ is dead in vain."*

According to Thayer's lexicon, the word *frustrate* means to set aside, disesteem, neutralize, nullify, make void, or reject. In other words, when I try to do things in my own strength, I nullify, reject, and neutralize the grace of God in my life. God does not take it away from me; through my unbelief, I choose to depend on my strength instead of His.

Focus on believing rather than on doing.

I may be so desperate that I "do right" for a while. Then one day I get tired of doing right, or I stir up that old desire again. Suddenly, I am faced with something that is stronger than my ability to do right, so I fall again. This is the cycle of the average believer: doing right, falling, struggling to summon the courage or desperation to try again, and eventually falling again.

If, however, I enter into the light and begin to affect my belief about my righteousness by accepting what Jesus says about me and acknowledging my righteousness through His finished work, then grace will begin to flood my heart. Then I will find God's ability (grace) to come out of my sin.

Our real problem, however, is that we simply do not believe that believing works. We look at and give heed to our works more than Jesus' finished work. Really, we have walked in our own abilities for so long that we do not know how to walk in His ability.

But you are on your way to finding the unlimited power of God. You are reading this book because you are sick and tired of just having what your ability can produce. You are looking for God, and you are going to find Him!

CHAPTER SIXTEEN

CONQUERING TEMPTATION

Sixteen

Conquering Temptation

In more than 20 years of ministry, I have noticed two very disturbing facts. First, most people never overcome their life-dominating problems. Many of the people I have known all my Christian life are still struggling with the same problems they have always had. In fact, they are so busy struggling with their problems, they cannot get on with life.

The second thing that disturbs me is that very few people know how to overcome temptation. Most of the people whom I have counseled, when faced with a temptation, do not have much hope of overcoming it. Many people are absorbed with worry, fear, or lust. They know that Jesus has promised victory, but they do not know how it comes.

The closest thing to victory that many believers ever see is simply tenacity. Tenacity is good. It is better than nothing, but it is not victory. Of course, you should resist sin however you can at this point. You do not want the pain of sin, but never think that sheer willpower is victory.

Tenacity and willpower involve using the best of our abilities. They will last as long we do not get weary. However, the first time we get tired, we will not be strong anymore. Or the first time we run into a problem that is stronger than our wills, we will not win. Or we may just see something that we want to give in to!

The worst aspect of using willpower is that we are still torn inwardly. We may not be giving in to sin outwardly, but inwardly we are struggling. That is not victory; eventually, we will give ourselves over to what controls our emotions.

Labor to Rest?

All it takes to end this struggle is to have our hearts established in righteousness. It is essential that we understand the paradox that the Bible describes in Hebrews 4:11: *"Let us labour therefore to enter into that rest."* This is a paradox that not even many grace teachers understand.

You see, you must labor to enter in. Laboring, however, is not what brings the change. Laboring effectively is not the victory, nor does it bring the victory. It does not say to labor for victory or change; it says to labor to enter into rest. Hebrews 4:10 explains what that means: *"For he that is entered into his rest, he also hath ceased from his own works, as God did from his."*

Hebrews 4:9 promises, *"There remaineth therefore a rest to the people of God."* There is a place where you cease from your own labors, yet you must labor to enter into this place, which is rest. When Jesus preached about the kingdom of God that was to come, He spoke of how difficult it would be to enter. He could not have been talking about how difficult it would be to born again, because that is clearly a free gift. Yet, on one hand, He would say, "All who believe." (See, for example, John 3:15–16.) Then He would say, *"Narrow is the way, which leadeth unto life"* (Matt. 7:14). What was the contradiction?

Lasting change comes by believing God.

In effect, Jesus was calling us out of this world's system. The same word that is used to denote this world's system is used also for the Jewish legal system—the law. Jesus was calling for us to transfer our citizenship. In order to change citizenship, we must change, learn, and abide by the change in the laws.

I cannot function by the same set of laws or principles in the kingdom of God that I did in the kingdom of darkness. Thus, the difficulty in entering in is not how hard it is to get saved; it is in how hard it is to give up my old ways of thinking. There has been a change of kingdoms, a change of priesthood, and a change in the system; therefore, I must change my views, opinions, and ideas. It will take an effort on my part to surrender my former beliefs. It will take an effort for my heart to be changed. That is the laboring.

Once I have changed my beliefs at the level of the heart, I will enter into rest. From that point on, every change that comes into my life will come from believing, never from doing. I will no longer win over sin by gritting my teeth, "bucking up," or making a great demonstration of willpower. Instead I will overcome with joy by my believing, but I must establish my heart in believing the truth.

Being Fully Persuaded

Although we have previously discussed persuading the heart, I want to touch on it again. The Bible says of Abraham in Romans 4:21, *"And being fully persuaded that, what he had promised, he was able also to perform."* Abraham was fully persuaded. That was the key to his continual confidence in God. A person who is not persuaded will waver.

In Romans 8:38–39, Paul testified to what he was persuaded about the love of God. He wrote:

For I am persuaded, that neither death, nor life, nor angels, nor principalities, nor powers, nor things present, nor things to come, nor height, nor depth, nor any other creature, shall be able to separate us from the love of God, which is in Christ Jesus our Lord.

In Romans 14:5, Paul explained that whatever you believe, you must be fully persuaded of in your own mind. *"One man esteemeth one day above another: another esteemeth every day alike. Let every man be fully persuaded in his own mind."*

He said in 2 Corinthians 5:11 that his ministry was a ministry of persuading men. *"Knowing therefore the terror of the Lord, we persuade men."* It was Paul's persuasion in God's power that made him able to endure imprisonment and hardship without fear. He said,

For the which cause I also suffer these things: nevertheless I am not ashamed: for I know whom I have believed, and am persuaded that he is able to keep that which I have committed unto him against that day. (2 Tim. 1:12)

The common denominator of all the people listed in the great "roll call of faith" was that they were persuaded; thus, they had faith. Hebrews 11:13 tells us that common denominator:

These all died in faith, not having received the promises, but having seen them afar off, and were persuaded of them, and embraced them, and confessed that they were strangers and pilgrims on the earth.

The very word *faith* in the original language of the Bible is part of a word that means to trust and to be persuaded to trust. We do not have trust (faith) until we have been persuaded about God. That persuasion can come in many different ways. It can come from hearing others speak, from reading the Bible, from meditating on the Word of God, or from speaking the Word of God. It also can come as the Holy Spirit directs us into truth. We should incorporate every possible means of persuading our hearts.

I spent a number of years "confessing" the Word daily in prayer and worship as a way to establish my heart. However, I never regarded that as the source of my righteousness. When I did begin to feel self-righteous about my diligence, I either stopped for a while or changed my thinking (repented). Now, I would be totally misleading you if I said that my heart got established just because I decided to believe. I did decide to believe, but then I took every biblical step I could to get that belief into my heart.

As a result, changes that have come into my life have been effortless. I do not have to confess every day to walk in love. I do not have to confess every day to be healthy. I do not have to confess every day to have God's protection. However, there was a time that if I did not do that on a daily basis, my heart would not have been stable enough to endure.

You have to decide to believe.

Once my heart got established in an area, I no longer had to labor to enter into rest in that area. You see, growing in this life does not mean things get harder and harder. It means that things get easier and easier. I do not have as much disciplined prayer today as I did ten years ago, but I have more spontaneous fellowship and leadership from the Holy Spirit.

Temptation comes in when our hearts become moved in an area. When we move away from our confidence in Jesus' fulfillment, provision, or promise, we are headed for temptation. If, however, we are persuaded in Jesus when that temptation comes, then it is a very easy thing to conquer. It all happens at the heart level.

Questions That Win the Battle

Second Corinthians 10:3, which is so misquoted and misused, says, *"For though we walk in the flesh, we do not war after the flesh."* Remember, this is not a Scripture that talks about warring with the devil. This Scripture talks about warring with vain imaginations, and it goes on to describe those imaginations.

Verse 5 says, *"Casting down imaginations, and every high thing that exalteth itself against the knowledge of God."* Any thought that is not consistent with the knowledge of God is a vain imagination. It is a high thing, an idol, a graven image in your mind. It must be cast down. But as 2 Corinthians 10:4 says, *"For the weapons of our warfare are not carnal, but mighty through God to the pulling down of strong holds."* This warfare is not done with carnal or natural methods.

Again, we do not fight this fight with our natural strength or by screaming at the devil. Second Corinthians 10:5 says, *"And bringing into captivity every thought to the obedience of Christ."* What could this possibly mean? Does it mean I make every thought obey me? Does it mean I am going to make my thoughts obey Christ? What does it mean?

When a vain imagination rises up, it challenges who you are in Jesus. It challenges your ability to resist temptation and sin. It denies all that Jesus came to give you. The real question you must ask yourself when you are tempted is this: "Did Jesus conquer this sin at His resurrection?" In other words, did Jesus' obedience bring Him victory over this sin? The answer is, obviously, yes!

> It is impossible to sin when you feel righteous.

The next issue that must be settled, then, is this: "Am I in Jesus? If I am in Jesus, if I am a joint heir of all He received, then I, too, have victory over this sin. I have His righteousness. I have His grace (ability); therefore, I am free from this temptation."

As I begin to acknowledge Jesus' victory over sin and the fact that I am in Him and am righteous, grace always comes to make me able to live above sin. I walk away from that sin with no desire for it, because the grace of God flows through my being. I feel the righteousness that abides in me.

This acknowledging of truth affects my heart. As I acknowledge who Jesus is in me, absolute victory comes. Philemon 1:6 says it this way:

> *That the communication* [the sharing, the living, the walking out] *of thy faith may become effectual* [effective] *by the acknowledging* [verbally and mentally] *of every good thing which is in you in Christ Jesus.*

You do not have to be afraid of temptation or sin ever again. You do not have to live the rest of your life struggling with your life-dominating problems. You can find out what it means to be free indeed.

Do whatever it takes to establish your heart in your identity in Jesus. I know of no better tool than *The Prayer Organizer,* but whatever you do, do not make that your righteousness. Do not get into law about persuading your heart; just get on with the process.

There is a new world, a new life, out there waiting for you. Dimensions of peace and joy yet to be explored are beyond your wildest dreams. Jesus died to give them to you, but you must believe in your heart. Otherwise, they cannot affect your life.

CHAPTER SEVENTEEN

GRACE TO CHANGE

Seventeen

Grace to Change

We got saved for one of two reasons: either we did not want to go to hell or we wanted to change. Hopefully, if avoiding hell was your only reason initially, you have since developed new motivation.

For me, it was a little of both. I did not want to go to hell. There was, however, a much stronger need in me. It was the need to change. I was sick of who I was, what I was doing, and the way I was.

I knew in my heart that God was the only One who could help me. However, I did not want to become like most Christians I had seen. What they had was more of a disease or addiction than a life.

As a child, I lived at the theater on Saturday afternoons. I had seen all the great movies about Bible characters. I had seen *The Ten Commandments* and was thrilled with the story of Samson. I wanted to know the God those heroic biblical people knew. He was different from the God whom Christians knew. He was real and powerful. He could change lives.

All my life I wanted to know God, although there was nothing in my behavior to indicate that. I went to church only a handful of times in my entire life before being saved. Everyone who knew me thought I was an atheist. Christians were afraid to witness to me. The ones who did witness to me did not give witness to the risen

Lord who loved me and wanted to help me. They gave witness to the god of their imagination, the one who hated me the way I was and who demanded that I change with my own ability.

For years I prayed every night. I told God that I did not want to die and go to hell. I told Him every night that I wanted help. I wanted to change; I just knew that I could not do it in my own power. I had tried and failed too many times.

One day while driving along with a musician friend, God found a way into my life. This man's cousin had been saved and had witnessed to him. My friend was cursing and criticizing everything his cousin had said to him; but in the midst of all the profanity and criticism, he quoted a few of the Scriptures that he had heard. That was enough for me.

After I let him out of my car, I felt those Scriptures burning in me like fire. The Bible says in John 16:8, *"And when he is come, he will reprove the world of sin, and of righteousness, and of judgment."* The moment He had some truth to work with in me, the Holy Spirit did His job. It is important to note that this is how the Holy Spirit relates to the world, not the church.

Knowing the Truth Set Me Free

The Living Bible makes this point so understandable. It reads,

And when he has come he will convince the world of its sin, and of the availability of God's goodness [righteousness], *and of deliverance from judgment. The world's sin is unbelief in me; there is righteousness available because I go to the Father and you shall see me no more; there is deliverance from judgment because the prince of this world has already been judged.*
(John 16:8–11)

The Holy Spirit had to convince me that because of Jesus, I could be freed from sin and have righteousness. When I prayed, I was surrendering my life to Him to change it in whatever way He wanted, because I knew I could not change. That admission of inability and dependence on His ability caused the greatest single change that ever took place in my life.

I did not do one thing to earn it. All I did was believe, pray, and trust. The consequent changes were totally effortless

No one's salvation can be earned.

on my part. I remember thinking, I need to test this new experience out to see if it is real. So I went to a party to see if I could resist all the temptations. I not only resisted them, but didn't even want to give in to any of them. A change had taken place in me that was totally separate from my ability or understanding.

I walked in great freedom for a number of years. I joined a little Baptist church that was within walking distance of my home. The pastor there was a wonderful man who really helped me. He laid a foundation in me that ultimately brought me into the truth I know today.

It was not very long until I realized I was a thorn in the side of the Baptists. You see, I had been baptized in the Holy Spirit. I was casting out devils and doing all sorts of things they did not believe in. So I began to search for another church.

The next church I became part of was a charismatic church. The pastor of this church was one of the best preachers I had ever heard. He was so persuasive. The only problem was, truth did not work very well for him.

Then I attended a charismatic Bible school. One of the things I soon noticed was that no one seemed to be able to get what they believed to work. There were a lot of sermons about all the reasons it did not work and all the things we had to do to make it work. The closer I listened, the more notes I took, and the more I believed what I was hearing, the less anything worked in my life.

It Is His Ability, Not Ours

I had become like the Galatian believers. Paul asked them, *"Are ye so foolish? having begun in the Spirit, are ye now made perfect by the flesh?"* (Gal. 3:3). They, like me, had begun this Christian life through the power of the Holy Spirit. But now they were attempting to finish this work by their own abilities (their flesh).

The Holy Spirit did not come into you to bring a few initial changes, then leave you on your own. As Philippians 1:6 says, *"Being confident of this very thing, that he which hath begun a good work in you will perform it until the day of Jesus Christ."* We are not saved by grace and made righteous by works. The Gospel reveals faith righteousness *"from faith to faith"* (Rom. 1:17).

Every change that needs to come into your life can come by the power of the Spirit of God, totally independent of your works. The same way you started this walk is the same way you finish this walk. Colossians 2:6 says, *"As ye have therefore received Christ Jesus the Lord, so walk ye in him."*

The Holy Spirit continues to help believers as they walk in faith.

If you are struggling with trying to change yourself, as I was, you have probably come to the place where your confidence to change is based on your own ability rather than trusting in God to make the changes. You have rendered Jesus non-effective by leaving the realm of grace.

Very few people ever give up on God. They give up on themselves. They give up on their abilities—which they should give up on. You gave up on your ability when you got saved. But you, like me, were slowly seduced back into entering into works, effort, and personal ability.

Paul said in Galatians 5:16, *"This I say then, Walk in the Spirit, and ye shall not fulfil the lust of the flesh."* The flesh always desires gratification—every kind of gratification. The Christian gratifies the flesh when he tries to be righteous in his own efforts. This removes us from grace (God's ability) and places us back in the realm of our own abilities.

Even though you are saved and have a new nature, your ability to resist sin is the same as it was before you were saved. You needed to be saved because you did not have the ability to live the way you wanted to live. If you go back to trusting in your own ability, you will just pick up where you left off; eventually, you will end up in the same place. Galatians 5:19–21 says,

Now the works of the flesh are manifest, which are these; Adultery, fornication, uncleanness, lasciviousness, idolatry, witchcraft, hatred, variance, emulations, wrath, strife, seditions, heresies, envyings, murders, drunkenness, revellings, and such like: of the which I tell you before, as I have also told you in time past, that they which do such things shall not inherit the kingdom of God.

When a person is in the flesh (relying on personal ability), these sins—the *"works of the flesh"*—begin to manifest themselves. Why? Because your flesh is not able to resist gratification on its own. You will find yourself in sin if you try to live in your own ability. The changes you are looking for will not be as difficult to make as you assume. I have seen thousands of people find immediate change with a few small adjustments in their believing.

Discover the simplicity of trusting in Christ.

In these remaining few pages, you will find the power of effortless change. By believing the truth, you will return to the simplicity of Christianity. You will rediscover how simple, easy, and joyous it is to know the Lord. You will realize what Jesus meant when He said,

Come unto me, all ye that labour and are heavy laden, and I will give you rest. Take my yoke upon you, and learn of me; for I am meek and lowly in heart: and ye shall find rest unto your souls. For my yoke is easy, and my burden is light.

(Matt. 11:28–30)

Chapter Eighteen

Touching the Heart

Eighteen

Touching the Heart

In order to fully understand man and his needs, one must understand the heart of man. As we have discussed before, all lasting change, good or bad, is the result of something happening in the heart. What we believe in our hearts determines everything that happens in our lives.

You may momentarily rise above or sink beneath the level of your heart, but you will always return to what you believe inside. Thus, your life today is not a product of what you do; it is a product of what you believe. Therefore, trying to cause change by changing what you are doing is like trying to redirect the wind with a fan. If you stand in the right place, it will feel like it is working, but it is only an illusion.

Just for the record, you should know that I am not discouraging you from making improvements on your behavior. It is admirable and responsible for a person to exhibit self-control. However, you must realize that it is not real, lasting change; neither is it your righteousness. The good feeling you have about the changes you make is little more than self-righteousness. You feel good because you are doing good. But that feeling will flee when you stop doing good. Faith righteousness abides, regardless of behavior.

Real Bible truth always penetrates and reveals our motives. As long as fear of judgment is present, we never know what our motives are. But liberty—exemption from the results—always exposes our hearts.

> *For the word of God is quick, and powerful, and sharper than any twoedged sword, piercing even to the dividing asunder of soul and spirit, and of the joints and marrow, and is a discerner of the thoughts and intents of the heart.* (Heb. 4:12)

When a person initially discovers faith righteousness and the gospel of peace, he is often surprised at what surfaces in his life. Once you remove the threat of punishment, what is in a person's heart is revealed. This message does not cause a person to sin; the sin is in his heart. This message will, however, reveal what is in his heart.

Your life is a product of what you believe.

For the first time, people begin to discover why they have been struggling. They find out that God has not failed them; they learn that the Word is true and will work. For the first time, the veil is lifted from their hearts. But it happens only when the threat of judgment is removed.

Why Did You Stop Sinning?

Now let's look a little deeper at discovering your heart's motives. Because of wrong teaching, believers tend to have a wrong view of sin and of God. We tend to view sin as those things that are pleasurable, but forbidden. In his research, Tony Robbins discovered that people will do all they can to avoid pain and experience pleasure.

Although I do not pretend to know what Mr. Robbins believes, I do know that he has discovered a biblical reality. God created man and placed him in a Garden called Paradise. That sounds like a very pleasurable experience. All man's needs were met. There was no lack, no suffering, no pain.

Because man did not trust God's integrity, though, he took things into his own hands. Every pain that has happened since the Garden of Eden has been introduced by man's wrong beliefs and behavior. Yet we are convinced that all our pain is God's way of dealing with us.

In Galatians 3:13, Paul said, *"Christ hath redeemed us from the curse of the law, being made a curse for us: for it is written, Cursed is every one that hangeth on a tree."* God did not want man to continue in pain and suffering, so He caused Jesus to experience all pain for us. God never intended that we would live in pain and suffering. We were created to live in the pleasure of total provision and in a completely positive relationship with God.

However, the average Christian's belief system denies this truth. We do not see sin as destructive and painful. We see it as a list of all the pleasurable things that God will not allow us to do. We consider living a godly life as dull, unfulfilling, limiting, and painful. This is why we habitually gravitate back to sin.

When we come under stress, or when hardship, pressure, or difficulties enter our lives, we begin to desire something pleasurable. Since we believe in our hearts that sin is pleasurable, we pursue sin instead of God. Then when the pain and destruction of sin begins to work in our lives, we think God is bringing that pain to bring us back in line. We will never conquer sin with this type of belief system.

Think back over your life. Think about all the things you stopped doing after you became a believer. Make a list of all those things. Then, beside that list, write down why you stopped doing each of those things. Really think this through.

Did you decide to stop doing those things because you saw that they were destructive; because they were bringing pain and suffering;

because they were the source of pain in your life? Or did you stop doing those things because you thought you had to in order to be accepted by God? Did you stop doing those things because you thought God would punish you if you did not stop?

If you stopped anything out of fear and have never changed that motivation, you are still struggling with that sin. Until you see that improper beliefs and sinful actions are the source of every pain in your life, you will never abandon those beliefs and actions.

If you consider sin as the pleasure you had to give up, but didn't want to; if you do not enjoy God and His Word and instead feel that they are the price you have to endure in order to avoid hell, then you will struggle forever. Only when you hear the message of peace with God do you allow what is really in your heart to surface. The sin that is in your heart will manifest itself when fear is removed.

At that point, you will find that you have not served, given, or changed because you enjoy a loving relationship with a good God, but because you are afraid of an angry God. Although it is some-what distressing to discover this, it is a first step to real victory.

Many times people come to me and say, "Jim, this message is not working." I always inquire, "What makes you think that?" They usually answer with something like, "Well, I don't tithe like I did before, and I find myself not wanting to do the things I did before. I don't come to church as often; I don't pray as

Your real emotions are revealed when fear is removed.

often," etc. I always respond like this: "It sounds like it is working to me." Of course, they always look shocked at my answer.

Then I start to question them about why they did all those things before. I always get answers like, "I gave because I was afraid I would come under the curse if I didn't. I prayed because I didn't be-lieve I would have God's protection if I didn't. I was regular at church so the pastor would think I was faithful." The real emotions behind anything a person stops or starts are revealed when fear is removed.

The beauty of this comes when, for the first time, a person can understand why he struggles with sinful thoughts and behavior. It is so freeing to know that God has not let you down. You find out that you are not a totally weak failure. You discover that you have just been living life out of your heart.

The Way to Change

Bringing about change is not as difficult as it may seem. It all revolves around repentance. Remember, the word *repentance* literally means a change of mind. What you change your mind from is not nearly as important as what you change your mind to. Repentance deals with what you start believing, not what you stop doing. Doing is controlled by believing. When you change your believing, your doing will change effortlessly.

Start by accepting the fact that you are righteous in Jesus. Think on it, say it aloud with your mouth, remind yourself of it regularly. Because you are righteous through Jesus, you must accept that God loves and accepts you. You do not need to do one thing to be accepted by God—if Jesus is your righteousness.

Unless you believe you are righteous, you will be limited to

Grace reigns through righteousness.

your ability. *"That as sin hath reigned unto death, even so might grace reign through righteousness unto eternal life by Jesus Christ our Lord"* (Rom. 5:21). If you believe you are righteous, God's ability will come forth—after you decide in your heart what you want in your life.

The greatest way I know to affect our hearts about sinful beliefs and behavior is to make it all plain to ourselves. Remember, every pain in your life today is the result of something you believe or something you are doing. And since we are righteous, we never approach change from the perspective of right and wrong. Making decisions based on what is right or wrong can deceive us and lead us into destruction.

Paul said in 1 Corinthians 6:12, *"All things are lawful unto me, but all things are not expedient: all things are lawful for me, but I will not be brought under the power of any."* The word *"expedient"* means profitable, suitable, helpful, and beneficial. If we are free from the law, then we are righteous. We do not make decisions based on what will make us righteous by the law. We are righteous by Jesus.

If I realize that sin is what brings pain into my life; if I realize that truth is the source of all fulfillment and joy; if I realize that I have it in my power to experience the good things of God by my decision making, then I will make my decisions from a totally different motive base. I realize that what I choose to believe and do affects my joy and pleasure in this life—and I will decide for truth.

Make a list of every pain in your life. Then link it to the belief or behavior that is bringing that pain. Do everything you can to see the belief or behavior that is bringing that pain. Then list all the pleasure that could be derived from walking in truth.

I have seen people get up from the counseling table free from life-dominating problems after just one session by implementing this simple procedure. Once you see the source of pain as it really is, and the source of potential pleasure that comes from operating in truth, you will make an absolute decision in your heart for righteousness. When that decision is made, the grace (ability) of God will flow forth from your heart to make you able to live what you have decided.

You could be just minutes away from turning your life around. Stop what you are doing, lay this book down, and make your lists. The change you desire is nearer than you think. You do not have to consider your past track record, your failures, or your ability. This change, like the greatest change that has ever come into your life, will come by believing the truth and experiencing the power of God.

GRACE COMPLETED

Nineteen

Grace Completed

Regardless of how many times we define grace as God's ability, despite how often we point to grace as the ability to come out of sin, regardless of the fact that the Bible says law is the power of sin—*"The sting of death is sin; and the strength of sin is the law"* (1 Cor. 15:56)—no matter that the Bible says being free from law and under grace is the one and only reason we are free from the dominion of sin—*"For sin shall not have dominion over you: for ye are not under the law, but under grace"* (Rom. 6:14)—there are still those who keep saying that to abandon the law is to encourage sin.

There are those today, just as in Paul's day, who say that preaching grace is saying it is all right to sin. Personally, I have never heard a person preach grace that said it was all right to sin; but we, like Paul, have been accused of that.

A Believer Sins Because He Wants To

The carnal mind cannot conceive of being free from law and not sinning. The carnal mind cannot grasp the power of faith righteousness. As one Pentecostal preacher confided to me, "If I were free from the law, you can't believe what I would do!" There have been many cases of people who, having heard about freedom from law, begin to live loose, destructive lives. But no one ever told them that it was all right for them to sin. No one ever encouraged those people to sin.

People who sin do it because they want to. They believe that sin will bring them pleasure. Now, for the first time, the person counseling them knows why they have been unstable and depressed for years. Truth did not send them over the edge; it revealed what was in their hearts. If we will deal with our beliefs now before they become behaviors, we can bring about permanent change from the inside out.

It is all right to deal with behavior from the proper perspective. The Bible calls it sowing and reaping. Sowing and reaping affect us on the horizontal plane—where we live. It does not mean that we sow something and God causes us to reap; rather, our actions cause us to reap the consequences in our lives.

People should know the effects that sin will have in their lives. They should know and identify all the destruction in their lives and associate it with the sin they believe or commit. They should never be led to believe that God is bringing the pain. As a preacher of grace, I must be very clear about the destructive results of sin.

Grace Brings the Power to Change

When some people first hear the message of truth, they simply throw off the law. There is usually a great freedom that is initially realized by the freedom from performance. But to stop at being free from the law will not bring the fulfillment and joy we seek.

Simply being free from law is no better than being under law. Freedom from the law will not change you. It will free you from the fear of judgment, which is good, but it will not bring the power to change. Therefore, we are left with our previous frustration.

When we were saved, we received a new nature. That nature has the same desires as the Spirit Himself. That nature longs for, craves, even lusts to be fulfilled. We have been predestined to be conformed to the likeness of Jesus; there is a craving in us for change. We cannot be satisfied to stay as we are.

Grace compels us to live in all godliness.

Righteousness gave us our identities, our new natures, our standing with God, and our new desires. But grace gives us the power to live godly lives and thereby fulfill those new desires. Titus 2:11–12 says,

> *For the grace of God that bringeth salvation hath appeared to all men, teaching us that, denying ungodliness and worldly lusts, we should live soberly, righteously, and godly, in this present world.*

Grace teaches us to deny ungodliness and to live in righteousness. Grace will not produce a lax attitude toward sin or ungodliness; grace compels us to live in all godliness.

Go for Grace

I recently had a discussion with a pastor who believed the message of grace but was struggling with some attitudes. Someone had come into his church and preached the grace message. This guest preacher never really said anything that was not true; yet, through overemphasizing freedom and underemphasizing responsibility, it was easy for people to misunderstand the message.

A man in this pastor's church had been up and down, on and off, for years. Upon hearing the message of grace, he "copped an attitude." He became almost arrogant in talking about his freedom from law. This man's past track record, along with a very offensive attitude, turned many people off to the grace message.

As we discussed this situation, I asked, "Was the guy a problem before he heard this message?" The answer was yes! Then this message did not cause the problem; it just gave him a new issue with which to display his bad attitude. There will always be people who misuse every message they hear. Yet we cannot throw away or be afraid of Bible truth because of the way a small number of people interpret it.

Neither can we try to keep people under law for fear of what they will do when they are freed from it. If law was going to change them, they would be changed. Look around. It has been those preachers who have preached law the strongest who have fallen. It did not work for them, and it is not working for you. We

Believing in faith righteousness makes grace work.

should quit preaching law, but at the same time we should preach grace responsibly.

If a person believes in faith righteousness, grace will come, and he will change. That person may not change according to your time table, but he will change. He may not change into what you want him to be, but he will change into what God wants him to be.

Remember, it is not believing in the doctrine of grace that makes grace work. It is believing in faith righteousness that makes grace work. One must believe that he is righteous through the Lord Jesus for grace to empower him.

A person cannot believe he is righteous and seek to live an unrighteous life. It also does not mean that he will never fall. It does mean that he will always desire righteousness, and he will always believe that he can live righteously. He will never run from God in fear; he will run to God in trust.

As righteousness is established in our hearts, sin loses all its power. We will rise above our fears of sin. We will rise above our desires for sin. Very little of our time and effort will revolve around trying to get victory. Instead, our lives will begin to revolve around the Person who has given us the victory. We will fall in love with our Savior and Lord. We will live our lives out of our relationship with God.

CHAPTER TWENTY

EFFORTLESS CHANGE

Twenty

Effortless Change

All lasting change is effortless. If change comes about by our efforts, then that change will last only as long as we put forth effort. The moment we stop putting forth effort, the change we made will stop. When we get tired, angry, or discouraged, or experience any negative emotions, we may stop putting forth effort. Then we are right back where we started.

Lasting change comes about by believing. Yet the church really does not believe that believing works. Instead, we trust in doing. However, Jesus said that if we would believe, we would do the works of God. *"Then said they unto him, What shall we do, that we might work the works of God? Jesus answered and said unto them, This is the work of God, that ye believe on him whom he hath sent"* (John 6:28–29). He has finished the work. Our job is to believe and thereby receive the benefits of that finished work (His doing).

Remember, however, that while change itself is effortless, changing your beliefs is not effortless. You must spend time in the Word of God and in fellowship with God to bring about a change in your believing. You may be required to change churches in order to change the input you are receiving. There will be a laboring to enter this rest, but that laboring will not change you. It is the truth you believe that will bring about the needed changes.

We Are Sons

First John 3:2 says, *"Beloved, now are we the sons of God, and it doth not yet appear what we shall be: but we know that, when he shall appear, we shall be like him; for we shall see him as he is."* John was writing to a group of people who, among other things, had been influenced to believe that if you were not flawless, you were not really saved.

He began this verse by saying, *"Now are we the sons of God."* We are not still becoming sons. It was understood in Bible times that to be a son meant you were an heir. And, if you were an heir, you had full privileges. We are sons of God by believing on and partaking of eternal life through the finished work of Jesus. Paul made this clear in Galatians 4:7: *"Wherefore thou art no more a servant, but a son; and if a son, then an heir of God through Christ."*

John also said, *"It doth not yet appear what we shall be"* (1 John 3:2). The word *"appear"* is means to reveal or manifest. He was saying, although we are sons this very moment, that fact may not be manifest. You see, they had the same problems we have. They were saved, their spirits were made perfect, but outwardly they might not have been living perfectly.

Not having it revealed on the outside does not mean it is not true on the inside. The Gnostics were trying to disqualify the early believers from their inheritance because they had not yet become the finished product of perfection.

John continued, *"When he shall appear, we shall be like him."* This is a passage that usually is applied to the Second Coming, and it undoubtedly has its ultimate reality in the Second Coming. But the word *"appear"* is the same here as it was in the first part of the verse. It means to reveal or manifest.

Thus, it would be safe to translate that passage in this way: "When Jesus is revealed or made manifest, we will become like

Him." Here is the point: we do not need to wait until the Second Coming to have a revelation of Him. We can find that now by studying the Scriptures.

This passage goes on to say that it is seeing *"him as he is"* that brings about that change. So if I can see Jesus as He is now, I can change now, and it will be effortless change. It will be a change that comes about by a change in my believing. That change in my believing comes about because I see Jesus as He is. How powerful! How wonderful! How easy!

How Do You See God?

Seeing Jesus changes us.

One of the greatest hindrances to bringing about positive change is the way we see God, the way we see Jesus. Try as you may, if you have a negative view of God, you cannot become a positive Christian. If you see God as angry, you will be angry. If you see God as vengeful, you will be full of vengeance. If you see God as fault-finding, you will be fault-finding. You are continually being changed into the image of the God you believe in. That change happens without effort on your part. It is happening by the power of believing.

Very early in my Christian walk, the Lord spoke to my heart about reading the Gospels. I knew that unless I read the Gospels regularly, I would lose touch with who Jesus really was and what He was really like. It would be very easy to get wrapped up in the theological issues of the Epistles and lose touch with Jesus. We must remember that we are called into a relationship with a Person, not a doctrine. I must know that Person in order to have a relationship with Him.

If I ever formulate a doctrine from the Epistles that is contrary to the life that Jesus lived, it cannot be true. So much of accepted church doctrine not only denies the finished work of the Cross but is also totally inconsistent with Jesus' life and ministry.

Jesus came and revealed God. The Jews had lost touch with God. Through the development of their theological system, they had totally perverted who God is. They had reduced God to a set of rules and regulations. They did not see Him as a God of love who was working to restore man; they saw Him as angry, mean, fault-finding, legalistic and even cruel. Jesus depicted something totally different.

Hebrews 1:3 in the *New International Version* says of Jesus, *"The Son is the radiance of God's glory and the exact representation of his being."* Jesus was an exact representation of God while here on earth. When you look at the life of Jesus, the way He treated people, you see nothing but love, kindness, and mercy. The only hard words Jesus had

To become godly, imitate Jesus.

for anyone were for the religious leaders, who were turning people away from God.

If I am to become like Him, it is essential that I see Him as He is. I can do that by looking at how He related to people. He met their needs. He healed the sick. He extended mercy. He was love personified. His life shows me the nature and character of the Father.

For you to understand the dynamics of personal change, you must examine what you believe about God. You will never personally rise above what you believe about God. Let's look at some Scriptures where you can honestly examine your beliefs about God. You may have some beliefs of which you are unaware.

We Become like the God We Believe In

First, let's resolve a few basic ideas. Do you believe you are supposed to be godly or Godlike? In other words, should you live like God? Should you show the nature and character of God? The answer is obvious: yes! We are called to be like Jesus. He is the exact representation of the Father, so we should be Godlike in our lifestyles.

Therefore, it is safe to say that anything God would require of me would be something that He would do. He would not require me to have one standard and Him have another. Since He is God, He would not require me to live in a higher standard of righteousness than He lives in. In other words, I am not more righteous than God.

In Matthew 5:43, Jesus said, *"Ye have heard that it hath been said, Thou shalt love thy neighbor, and hate thine enemy."* He starts by pointing out that it is not written. God never said this. It had only been said that He said this.

He continues in Matthew 5:44 by saying, *"But I say unto you, Love your enemies, bless them that curse you, do good to them that hate you, and pray for them which despitefully use you, and persecute you."* We all believe this is the way we should live. But if you really believe this is the way you should live, it may reveal some contradictions in your belief system.

How do you think God feels about His enemies? You probably think He is full of anger toward them. But if He requires you to love your enemies while He hates His enemies, then this is an area where you are not being like God. This would be an area where you are more righteous than God. But you know that cannot be true. No man is more righteous than God. However, if we believe we should love our enemies but it is all right for God to hate His enemies, then we have a problem in our belief systems.

Next Jesus says, *"Bless them that curse you."* What do you really believe God would do to a person who cursed Him? You know you would expect God to kill or, at least, punish him. Yet you are required to bless such a person. The word *"bless"* means to speak favorably, to be kind.

Then Jesus says, *"Do good to them that hate you."* Now we know God would not do good to someone who hated Him—would He? Why would He require you to be more righteous than He? If He said for you to do good to those who hate you, it is because that is what He does to those who hate Him.

Matthew 5:45 in *The Living Bible* goes on to say, *"In that way you will be acting as true sons of your Father in heaven."* We are acting like God only when we do these things, because that is how God relates to man. The remainder of verse 45 says, *"For he maketh his sun to rise on the evil and on the good, and sendeth rain on the just and on the unjust."* God does not withhold sunshine from the crops of the wicked. Neither does He withhold rain from them.

We have mistakenly thought that wrath would cause people to repent and turn to God. A quick glimpse at the book of Revelation reveals that wrath causes people to curse God and refuse to repent. (See Revelation 16:9.) What does cause people to repent? Romans 2:4 identifies the goodness of God as being His tool for bringing people to repentance. *"Or despisest thou the riches of his goodness and forbearance and longsuffering; not knowing that the goodness of God leadeth thee to repentance?"*

You become like the God you believe in.

If you thought that rejection would make people repent, if you thought that was the tool God was using, if you really believed that was how God responded to people, you would reject people who had problems. Why? You become like the God you believe in.

If you saw someone curse God, you would probably feel obligated to show that person wrath and indignation. Why? You assume that is how God responds. But according to these passages, God does not respond that way.

You see, we have an entire view of God that is unscriptural. Yet because those are our beliefs, we are being transformed into that likeness. When a person desires acceptance, he will conform to the image of the one from whom he desires acceptance. Teenagers do it every day. They grow their hair long, get tattoos, and wear a certain kind of clothing to become like those from whom they seek acceptance. Likewise, we become like the image of the God from whom we desire acceptance.

The law insisted, *"Ye shall make you no...graven images"* (Lev. 26:1). Today we do not go to the woods, cut down a tree, and fashion it into a god to worship. Yet we have idolatry as rampant as it ever was. The idol that we exalt is the vain imagination we have of God.

We construct a concept of God that is different from the revelation that Jesus showed us. We try to relate to and see God through the understanding of the old covenant. Or we have a view of God that some preacher or relative has given us. No matter how that belief comes, it becomes an idol in our minds that isolates us from a relationship with the true and living God. It dictates what we will become.

When you believe in a God who really loves, you will really love.

In order to see God, you must look at Him through the life of Jesus. Go to the Gospels and look at Jesus' life and ministry. Do not try to know Him through His teachings alone; know Him through His life and ministry as well.

When you believe in a God who is always patient and longsuffering, you will find yourself becoming patient and longsuffering. When you believe in a God who sees you as holy and sanctified, you will see people as holy and sanctified. When you believe in a God who really loves, you will really love.

CHAPTER TWENTY-ONE

THE TRUTH ABOUT GOD

Twenty-one

The Truth about God

As you can see, the truth about God has been hidden from the church. It is not the devil who is killing us as much as it is our belief systems. If we believed the truth, the devil could never touch our lives. Screaming at the devil will not change your problems; believing the truth will change your problems.

We must be able to read Scripture without twisting it. We must be able to pick up our Bibles and hear God instead of hearing man. You see, we, like the Jews, render the Word powerless through our traditions. In Mark 7:8–9, 13, Jesus upbraided them for listening to man more than to God.

> For laying aside the commandment of God, ye hold the tradition of men....And he said unto them, Full well ye reject the commandment of God, that ye may keep your own tradition....Making the word of God of none effect through your tradition, which ye have delivered: and many such like things do ye.

We are full of tradition more than we are of truth. We are influenced more by man than we are by God. We accept whatever the preacher says, based on his power of persuasion. Many people who heard Apollos preach preferred his message over Paul's. The problem, however, was that Apollos was not even saved when he first began to preach. He was simply a better preacher. (See Acts 18 and 1 Corinthians 3.)

Tradition or Truth?

When I gave my life to the Lord, I made two commitments. First, I promised I would never "play church." Second, I committed to believe only about God what I could find for myself from the Bible. Many times in my life, I have had to repent, return to that commitment, and purge myself of the tradition I had picked up along the way.

When I was healed of a kidney disorder, it happened only after I got my believing straight. While I was praying one day, the Lord spoke to my heart and said, "You don't see Me as I am." I was greatly offended. I said, "Lord, I have refused to give in to tradition. I have been willing to be different. I have suffered reproach because I would not conform." He simply replied, "You don't see Me as I am." The third time He added more. "In the area of healing, you don't see Me as I am. You see Me as you have been influenced to believe I am."

Are you full of tradition or truth?

I was shocked to realize all the false stipulations I had placed on healing. I had accepted the word of men. What made it so bad was that these were men who could not get healed themselves. I had been influenced to see healing the way they saw it, because they presented it in a way that was reasonable and logical. Regardless of how appealing it was to my carnal mind, it was not true, and it did not work.

I can look back at times in my early walk with God when I became hard and mean. It really seemed that the closer I got to God, the meaner I got. I found myself being critical and fault-finding. I was intolerant of people and their problems. I had no compassion for people; I just had a set of standards I thought they should live up to. As I look back, I now realize that I was becoming just like the God I believed in. I was not drawing closer to God; I was becoming closer to my false image of God.

How could I read the Bible and be so confused? How could I look at the life of Jesus and end up with a doctrine that made me act so contrary to everything Jesus ever did? The answer is simple. I found in the Bible exactly what I was looking for.

How Do You Set Your Sail?

I once heard a story about a young boy who was standing on the edge of the sea. He was amazed that the wind blew in one direction, yet the boats moved in every direction. He looked up at the old man beside him and asked how this could happen. The old man replied, "By the setting of the sail." You see, it does not matter which way the wind blows. It is the way you set your sail that will determine the direction of your boat.

Set your sail to determine your direction.

Likewise, how you see God determines what you will look for in Scripture. It determines how you set your sail. Regardless of what the Word says, you have predetermined how you will interpret what you read.

Keep in mind, Jesus read the same Scriptures that the Jews read. Yet He found a different God. They found judgment; He found mercy. They saw sickness as God's punishment; Jesus saw it as oppression of the devil. (See Acts 10:38.) They thought man should serve the law; Jesus taught that the law should serve man.

Jesus gave us the best rule for interpreting Scripture in Matthew 22, when the Pharisees came to Him. Although they were not sincere in their question, He was very sincere in His answer. They asked Him which commandment was the greatest. Jesus not only answered that question, but also gave them the next greatest commandment. Based on these two commandments, He then made this astounding statement: *"On these two commandments hang all the law and the prophets"* (v. 40).

In essence, Jesus was saying that all the commandments would be satisfied if these two were fulfilled. He also was saying something more: all the commandments must be interpreted in light of these two commandments. What were these two commandments that provide our reference for all interpretation?

> *Jesus said unto him, Thou shalt love the Lord thy God with all thy heart, and with all thy soul, and with all thy mind. This is the first and great commandment. And the second is like unto it, Thou shalt love thy neighbor as thyself.* (Matt. 22:37–39)

Everything I believe must be interpreted in light of these two commandments. In other words, if what I believe does not make me love God and people more, it is not true. Likewise, if I just did these two things, I would fulfill every expectation that God has ever had for me.

Look at your belief system. Does everything you believe make you love God and love people? If what you believe makes you afraid of God or critical and fault-finding with others, it is not true. If you interpret any Scripture in a way that violates this principle, then you can never see God as Jesus did.

As I have done many times, you may need to sort through your beliefs and ask, "Does what I believe about this make me love God and love people?" If not, you must change what you believe. If you do not understand a passage in light of this interpreting procedure, don't worry about it. In due time, God will give you understanding.

Now that you have finished this book, you have all you need to change. Take these principles before God. Apply them to your life. Do not accept them merely because I wrote them. Check them with the Scriptures. Put them to the test, and see if they work.

BIBLIOGRAPHY

Adams, Jay E. *Competent to Counsel.* Grand Rapids: Baker, 1976.

Cremer, Herman. *Biblio-Theological Lexicon of New Testament Greek.* Edinburgh: T & T Clark Ltd., 1895.

Kittel, Gerhard, and Gerhard Friedrich, eds. *Theological Dictionary of the New Testament.* Geoffrey W. Bromiley, trans. Grand Rapids: William B. Eerdmans, 1985.

Lenski, R. C. *The Interpretation of St. Paul's Epistle to the Romans.* Minneapolis: Ausburg, 1936.

Phillips, J. B., trans. *The New Testament in Modern English.* New York: Macmillian, 1972.

Strong, James. *Strong's Exhaustive Concordance.* Grand Rapids: Baker, 1972.

Thayer, Joseph H., trans. *A Greek-English Lexicon of the New Testament.* Grand Rapids: Baker, 1977.

Vaughn, Curtis, ed. *The Word: The Bible from 26 Translations.* Grand Rapids: Baker, 1988.

ABOUT THE AUTHOR

Almost thirty years ago, James Richards found Jesus and answered the call to ministry. His dramatic conversion and passion to help hurting people launched him onto the streets of Huntsville, Alabama. His mission was to reach teenagers and drug abusers.

Before his salvation, James was a professional musician with all the trappings of a worldly lifestyle. More than anything, he was searching for real freedom. Sick of himself and his empty pursuits, he hated all that his life had become. He turned to drugs as a means of escape and relief. Although he was desperate to find God, his emotional outrage made people afraid to tell him about Jesus. He sought help, but became more confused and hopeless than before. He heard much religious talk, but not the life-changing Gospel.

Through a miraculous encounter with God, James Richards gave his life to the Lord and was set free from his addictions. His whole life changed! Now, after years of ministry, Dr. Richards still believes there's no one God can't help, and there's no one God doesn't love. He has committed his life to helping people experience that love. If his life is a model for anything, it is that God never quits on anyone.

Dr. Richards—author, teacher, theologian, counselor, and businessman—is president and founder of Impact Ministries®, a multi-faceted, international ministry committed to helping those whom the church has not yet reached. He is on the cutting edge of what works in today's society. He is president and founder of Impact International School of Ministry, Impact International Fellowship of Ministers, Impact Treatment Center, Impact of Huntsville Church, and Impact International Publications®. Thousands have been saved, healed, and delivered every year through his worldwide crusades and pastors' seminars.

With doctorates in theology, human behavior, and alternative medicine, and an honorary doctorate in world evangelism, Dr. Richards is also a certified detox specialist and drug counselor, as well as a trainer for the National Acupuncture Detoxification Association (NADA). His uncompromising yet positive approach to the Gospel strengthens, instructs, and challenges people to new levels of victory, power, and service. Dr. Richard's extensive experience in working with substance abuse, codependency, and other social/emotional issues has led him to pioneer effective, creative, Bible-based approaches to ministry that meet the needs of today's world.

More than anything else, Dr. Richards believes that people need to be made whole by experiencing God's unconditional love. His message is simple, practical, and powerful. His passion is to change the way the world sees God so that they can experience a relationship with Him through Jesus.

He and his wife, Brenda, reside in Huntsville, Alabama. They have five daughters and ten grandchildren.

To find out more about Dr. Jim Richards, go to these websites: www.heartphysics.com or www.impactministries.com.

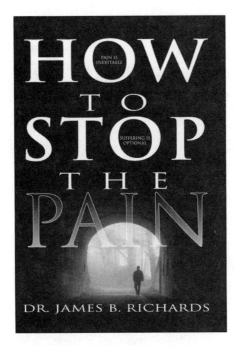

How to Stop the Pain
James B. Richards

You've been wounded, and you just can't seem to heal. You try to get on with your life, but you're stuck in the same old spot. You forgive, but you can't forget! Every day the pain you try to bury is exhumed. It cripples your relationships with others, God, and life itself. It destroys your ability to pursue your dreams. This paradigm-shattering book will free you from the forces that would turn you into a victim. Dr. James Richards will lead you step-by-step through a simple process that will free you from the pain of the past and protect you from the pain of the future. Discover the emotional freedom that everyone wants but few experience.

ISBN: 978-0-88368-722-2 • Trade • 208 pages

WHITAKER
HOUSE

www.whitakerhouse.com

A Healing Touch:
The Power of Prayer
Melanie Hemry

We all want prayers that move the hand of God. We want to be used and blessed and effective for the kingdom of God. But when someone says "intercessor," we balk, we run, we thank God that it's not our gift or our calling….But it is.

Melanie Hemry will challenge everything you ever believed about prayer. She will introduce you to a new kind of prayer—the soul-stirring, world-shaking, life-giving *prayer* that this world so desperately needs.

If you've been searching for God's presence, if you feel a deep need for unsaved souls, or even if you're just worried about the state of the world today, Melanie Hemry has the answer. As a former ICU nurse and prayer warrior, she is qualified to give you the heart transplant you need. You will not walk away from this book unchanged.

ISBN: 978-0-88368-780-2 • Trade • 192 pages

www.whitakerhouse.com

10 Curses That Block the Blessing
Larry Huch

Have you been suffering with depression, family dysfunction, marital unhappiness, or other problems and been unable to overcome them? Within the pages of this groundbreaking book, *10 Curses That Block the Blessing*, Larry Huch shares his personal experience with a life of anger, drug addiction, crime, and violence. He shows how he broke these curses and reveals how you can recognize the signs of a curse, be set free from generational curses, and restore your health and wealth. You don't have to struggle any longer. Choose to revolutionize your life. You can reverse the curses that block your blessings!

ISBN: 978-0-88368-207-4 • Trade • 272 pages

www.whitakerhouse.com

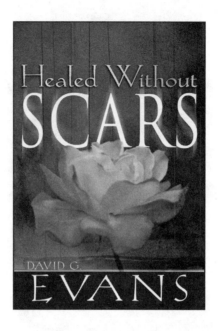

Healed Without Scars
David G. Evans

Have you been hurt by past disappointment, fear, rejection, abandonment, or failure? If so, you've probably learned that time doesn't necessarily heal all wounds. When pain from the past lingers in our lives and causes emotional scars, you need to understand that God is always ready to help you! Discover the path to personal wholeness, and find peace in the midst of life's storms. Renew your hopes and dreams, and experience a life of freedom and joy. For years, author David Evans has helped people from all walks of life learn how to live in victory. Let him guide you to a joyful life of wholeness in Christ as you learn that you can be *Healed Without Scars*!

ISBN: 978-0-88368-542-2 • Trade • 272 pages

www.whitakerhouse.com

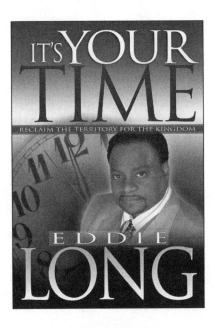

It's Your Time:
Reclaim Your Territory for the Kingdom
Eddie Long

Have we, as believers, allowed the world to silence us? By slowly eroding our rights to free speech…by passing laws saying that marriage isn't necessarily between a man and a woman…that murder is okay… that it's wrong to display the Ten Commandments… Is this really equality for all, except for Christians?

Join Eddie Long in reclaiming what has been lost. He will inspire you to rise up, take authority, and boldly assert your power as a believer. Discover how to redefine your life's purpose and vision while you raise your children to be godly leaders. Speak up, Christians! Now is the time for our unified voice to be heard, to take a stand together, and to stand firm. It's our time.

ISBN: 978-0-88368-783-3 • Hardcover • 192 pages

WHITAKER
HOUSE
www.whitakerhouse.com

The Principles and Power of Vision
Dr. Myles Munroe

Whether you are a businessperson, a homemaker, a student, or a head of state, best-selling author Dr. Myles Munroe explains how you can make your dreams and hopes a living reality. Your success is not dependent on the state of the economy or what the job market is like. You do not need to be hindered by the limited perceptions of others or by a lack of resources. Discover time-tested principles that will enable you to fulfill your vision no matter who you are or where you come from.

You were not meant for a mundane or mediocre life. Revive your passion for living, pursue your dream, discover your vision—and find your true life.

ISBN: 978-0-88368-951-6 • Hardcover • 240 pages

WHITAKER
HOUSE

www.whitakerhouse.com